Does God Hear Us?

Does God Hear Us?

Reflections on Christian Prayer Today

Andre Seve A. A.

Published in the United States by New City Press
206 Skillman Avenue, Brooklyn, New York 11211
©1990 New City Press, New York

Translated from the original French edition
Prier Aujourd'Hui by Richard Arnandex, FSC
©1988 Editions du Centurion, Paris, France

Cover design by Nick Cianfarani

Library of Congress Cataloging-in-Publication Data:

Sève André
    [Prier aujourd'hui. English]
    Does God hear us? : reflections on Christian prayer today /
  André Sève ; [translated by Richard Arnandez].
      p. cm.
    Translation of: Prier aujourd'hui
    ISBN 0-911782-82-6 : $7.95
    1. Prayer.   2. Title.
BV210.2.S47213 1990
248.3'2--dc20
                                          90-39972

Printed in the United States of America

TABLE OF CONTENTS

I.
PRAYER IS MAKING A COMEBACK

People long to pray; young and old alike. One kind of prayer has disappeared: the one involving formulas and obligations; but another kind is being born, a spontaneous kind. The two characteristics of today's prayer are: first, this freedom; and then also a deep desire for union with God. This book will speak a lot about union. Forms and times matter little, provided one gets to the essential thing: a conscious relationship with God. "You are there, and so am I."

From this desire for union there arises a multiplicity which is a fortunate thing, but sometimes it stirs up arguments. "Oh, those charismatics!" sigh some, while others exclaim: "Are you still saying the rosary?" or again, "Did you see that? They need to lie flat on their backs in order to pray!"

So, an investigation has to be made. Prayer is making a comeback, indeed; but what kind of prayer? We shall investigate, with a bias in favor of sympathetic curiosity. Even if, here and there, some reservations need to be made, there are a great many good things going on; and first of all, the seeking itself, and the eagerness which make it possible for a great many believers to find God's presence, and to discover the path which is right for them. If we begin by offering a panoramic view of the matter we shall not be tempted to confine prayer to a single type, and we shall be inclined to show ourselves sympathetic even when deep differences separate us.

Sunday Mass

This is the total prayer, the one most beloved. Those present are far less numerous now, but all are there voluntarily, and they participate. In the interviews I make for a Catholic daily newspaper, Mass is always cited as the religious event of the week.

Perhaps the greatest novelty is joy. Gone are the "strangers sitting side by side" whose only interest in others was made up of critical curiosity. People come to a ceremony which is both intimate and religious. The Pastor of a large city parish once told me, "When Mass begins each one gives his neighbor a big smile." And he insisted: "That way, Mass has already begun."

Another current characteristic of eucharistic celebrations is the desire to bring everything making up part of one's life into Christ's sentiments, and into his power. We come to thank God for the week just lived, and to start off on the new week of life granted to us. One saying assumes more and more importance: "Take and eat." Christ tells us: "Take my life, so as to live my life. Then you can give of yourselves, as I gave of myself."

These are some of the brighter aspects of the Mass. But there are shadows too. There is the problem of different generations. The older members remain very individualistic and conservative; the younger ones want things to get moving, and detest the idea of obligations.

Then there is the problem of the hymns, of universal prayer, of the eucharistic prayers. After a first part which is very lively and full of participation, the Mass suddenly changes into a solo by the celebrant.

And above all, the Mass still does not influence people's lives enough. The "take my life" is more of a dream than of a living reality. It was as they emerged from Mass that the first Christians felt themselves more ready to share their goods, and to face martyrdom.

Adoration of the Blessed Sacrament

Prayer before the tabernacle, which for a long time was the place to find union with God, seemed to have been abolished because of the closing of churches due to thieves and vandals. It even seemed condemned by the slogan: "Bread is not made to be adored, but to be eaten." Yet there is a return to the eucharistic presence, with clearer ideas about this adoration of the Host.

The Host is indeed the sign and the reality of Jesus who is offered as our food; but it is the consecration which makes him our food, not the fervor of the faithful, nor even the eating of the Host.

For the Lutherans, the eucharistic presence is bound up with "the use" of it, that is, the consecration, the distribution and the absorbing of the Host. They admit the real presence only during this series of events, and hence there can be no communion, or still less adoration, before or after the meal. The discussions that have taken place on this subject may have disturbed some; we need to reaffirm very strongly the clear Catholic position: so long as there is a consecrated host, Christ is present. This justifies not only preserving the Host for giving communion to the sick or to others, outside the time of Mass, but also the tabernacles in our churches, and the visits paid to the Blessed Sacrament, public adoration, benediction, and processions of the Most Blessed Sacrament.

Certainly, there was some exaggeration in loosening the ties between the Mass and the Host. All eucharistic devotion should remind us of Mass, and prepare us for Mass. I kneel before the tabernacle or the monstrance; I believe that Jesus Christ is there, but as my bread of life. "Take my life, to live my life." Perhaps I have come to tell him all about myself, to find his soothing presence, to pull myself together before him. Why not? Provided I quickly come to the eucharistic meeting properly so called: Jesus offering us his .active presence to make us live what the Mass wants to make us live: self-offering, self-sacrifice, and going out towards our brothers and sisters. What is once more drawing people to pray before the tabernacle is this invitation to give oneself like Jesus. Silent adoration makes it possible to listen. The Host is not a mute Christ; what he tells us re-echoes in his silence: "What am I for you?" and, "Do you love as I am asking you to love?" or again, "Where are you right now? really close to me, your Savior, or lost in your own worries?"

The prayer of the present moment

Formerly the breviary was that black book with gold edges seen in priests' hands at church and everywhere. It was his big concern. "I have to say my breviary." "I haven't finished my breviary yet." Sometimes it was a happy kind of prayer: the wealth of the psalms and readings, the feeling of being united with the prayer of the whole Church. But more often it was like forced labor, what with the Latin, the length of the office, the strict obligation . . . one could not omit even the slightest bit of it.

Along with the liturgical reform there appeared, in July, 1969, the new breviary, all in the vernacular, entitled *Christian Prayer* which many lay people adopted. They are rather less enthusiastic, and one can understand them, about the breviary in four volumes edited in 1980, and called *Liturgy of the Hours.* But there remains the new and double joy of praying the breviary now in the vernacular, and of seeing both priests and lay people joining in this prayer.

Prayer groups and prayer corners

It is not unusual to hear someone say: "I belong to a prayer group." This expression covers a considerable variety of set-ups:

The Biblical group

This is not a group that meets to study the Bible; it remains mostly dedicated to prayer, properly so called. Isolated, or connected with a larger movement, the Bible prayer group adopts a yearly program. The one I belong to decided to pray, successively, with the Psalms, then Genesis, the Canticle of Canticles, St. Mark, St. Luke, the Acts of the Apostles. Our monthly meetings last two hours. We begin by reading a passage which the members have meditated on during the previous month. In turn, each member expresses what this text has meant in his life: joy, prayer, trouble, questions, resolutions. This is a moving moment. Each speaker is heard with no interruptions. We take notice, often with emotion, of the Bible's diverse impact on believers, of what arises from their personal culture, their social environment . . . and from the Holy Spirit. Then the leader tries to answer the questions put, and a discussion begins. It closes by a fresh reading of the text, then come some minutes of quiet reflection, which permit us to go into the second part of the meeting: thirty minutes of silent prayer.

Silent prayer

Some groups gather for an entirely silent prayer, meditation made together which is begun and ended by a short vocal prayer, the reading of a text, some music or a song. The place is important: it is here that one can speak of a "prayer corner." This can be found anywhere: in a little studio, or in a big family mansion, in the oratory of a religious community, or even in a church, generally next to the tabernacle. On a carpet are placed some cushions or little benches. One or several large icons are displayed; candles too, and flowers, and a big Bible.

The Charismatic group

These gather as a rule for vigil services. I have just returned from one which lasted nearly three hours. Those present are a very mixed group, as regards age, social

*Does religious culture help people
to pray better?*

God always welcomes our simple good will, but he has given us intelligence we can use on everything, including prayer. By studying this topic in sessions and with books, what can we acquire?

—a high idea of prayer. Why should we pray? It would be very useful to dig deep into this "why?" at times when we lose both the taste for prayer and the courage to keep on praying.

—clear ideas on the results of prayer. How are we heard? How does it change us?

—means for breaking away from routine, the ever-present threat to prayer.

—finding greater depths in the forms of prayer we have adopted. For instance, look into the Rosary in its "gospel connections."

—discovering new forms of prayer.

—praying in line with our own changing personality; age is a factor; it may be time for us to modify our manner of praying. This does change, inevitably; we do well to realize this.

—through study we can strengthen the conviction that prayer demands, and will always demand, an apprenticeship.

condition, color. There was a lot of singing, of very simple and effective chants, which are sometimes rhythmical, and if so, there is much clapping to keep time, which I found rather mechanical. Someone prayed aloud and the assembly (I counted nearly two hundred people sitting on the floor or on chairs) punctuated his words with expressions like: "Blessed are you, Lord!" "Praise the Lord!" "Thanks!" "Pardon!" It was all very simple, warm, spontaneous and sincere. A priest read and commented on a passage of St. Paul. Then the prayer started again, but suddenly it became a murmured chant, very soft, and in several voices. For the first time since the beginning I felt myself touched, and I began praying too. Someone said something. I did not understand him, but another seemed to translate: "I am the light; I am thy light!" Then more prayers, for the sick, for a family having difficulties. The group broke up with great signs of friendship.

Rosary groups

I discovered the revival of the rosary when I was doing one of my interviews. The lady I was interviewing revealed to me with deep feeling the entire life of prayer and the simple but effective apostolate which was developing in a certain city, all starting from group recitation of the rosary. After the interview appeared, I got a large number of letters asking me how a similar prayer group could be launched.

What is it, really? Ten or so people get together in a group which meets in the home of one of them, to say the rosary.

"I went," my informant told me, "and I was especially struck by the quality of the silent moments. It all lasts an hour. The movement provides a small booklet which presents an episode in the gospel. We start by a prayer to the Holy Spirit and then one to Mary; we read the passage; the leader gives a commentary which is interrupted by silent moments when one can let the meaning of the text sink in. I had never practiced such silent moments to assimilate a text, and now I see that this is the real way of listening to the word, of encountering Jesus who is speaking to us today. After that there may be reflections applying the text to our lives; nothing artificial here! At the end there is a prayer of intercession, and then we recite the rosary." The original features are the very powerful link between Mary and the gospel, and also the manner of getting a group started, and of spreading the movement. You look for ten persons to start a group; and then these persons start other groups. The missionary angle of it is to dare to suggest this to people who don't go to church, or who do not seem interested in the gospel.

For the time being it all remains very feminine, but men too could be gotten interested. All that I hear about it stresses three great benefits: people make new friends; there are some who return to the practice of their faith; and the encounter with Jesus through Mary brings peace; Mary exercises her spiritual motherhood.

The Jesus prayer

It is also called "Prayer of Jesus," or "Prayer of the Heart." It started in the fourth century among the monks in Egypt, and developed mostly in the East (Mt. Sinai, Mt. Athos) and then in Russia. Together with the icons, it is part of the riches of our oriental brothers and sisters which has for some time now been attracting prayerful souls in the West, who seek a very simple type of spirituality. But we have to be careful about this simplicity, which can very easily be reduced to a gimmick. A formula is repeated: "Lord Jesus Christ, Son of God, have mercy on me a sinner." Right there the specialists begin to talk diversely. Some affirm that we have to use the whole formula, with its double meaning: an act of faith (Son of God), and the petition (have mercy on me). On Mt. Sinai this prayer brought about great affection for Jesus, but in a context of austerity and recollection. Later, at Mt. Athos, a more formalized piety invented a rather complicated technique, based on the "descent of the name into the heart," and on one's respiration: inhaling brought in Jesus (Jesus Christ, Son of God); and exhaling expelled all one's misery (have mercy on me, a sinner). Other theoreticians of this prayer refuse to have anything to do with these technical aspects, and concentrate on the name of Jesus alone.

So, the important thing is in fact the name, but it must be received into the heart. When one tries it, he finds this to be a prayer that soothes, arouses tender and humble sentiments. (Jesus!) As for myself, I did not like the "have mercy on me," but I saw that this gave me a desire to make progress. If I say "have mercy" it is because I realize what I am, and I'm not much. But I say "Jesus," and I know that he saves me. Whenever we get discouraged, it is because we really are not saying "Jesus," deep in our hearts.

None of this prayer should be immutable, mechanical, formalistic. After a while one finds oneself simply repeating "Jesus!" but with what a difference!

Praying with books, records, slides

These are prayers of a new kind, prayers composed by fervent poets. The first and most famous book of this kind was Michel Quoist's *Prayers*. After that there came a flood of imitations, which did not impress me much. But, little by little, I find a poem here and there that touches me. Everyone must keep open to the possibilities of the poems, prayers and songs that open the heart to the mysteries of our faith. The St. Louis Jesuits have played this role for some. For others, it has been the songs from the Weston Priory. The list continues to grow. One may not wish to pray with these modern prayers, but the fact is that some people use them as a springboard for their personal prayer, when they feel too dry, and when the quality of some of these texts inspires them.

I discovered the practice of "praying" with cassette tapes while travelling on some wretched roads in southern Madagascar, mile after monotonous mile. The missionary who was driving suggested that we pray using a cassette published by a Trappist monastery. The beauty of the singing, the clear and fervent enunciation of the texts were of such help even in spite of the heat and the fatigue, that I have seldom celebrated Morning and Evening Prayer any better.

Some of the new hymns may disconcert some people by the obscurity of their lyrics and their outlandish melodies. They are not meant for the majority but for small groups making a retreat or a prayer vigil. I have seen how some musicians made people pray with this sort of intimate intensity. First, he gave a very brief presentation of the song; then they listened to it for the first time. After that came a rather long commentary, technical, literary and spiritual, which aroused interest. Then they learned how to sing, perhaps only the refrain at first; it was a really nourishing experience.

Slides also have begun to appear in the world of prayer. But to move on from simple curiosity or the pleasure of seeing, to prayer properly so called, does not happen by itself. One needs to re-discover the purity of his sight. Just as there are distractions when one meditates, there are also distractions when one just looks; there are barriers and interferences which spoil our contemplation of the image, and prevent our having direct contact with it. Concretely, whoever organizes a prayer session using slides must first call for concentration and recollection, exterior silence and interior silence. Everything must go which might come between us and a given scene: flower, tableau or icon — namely, souvenirs, comparisons, judgments. Then the eye can feast itself on the image, and become truly contemplative. This peaceful looking (rare enough most of the time) and this close union with the image draws us inward. For instance, the picture of a sunrise, or of a person, can be transformed into an inner gaze on God. We make bad use as a rule of these "go-betweens" connecting us and God; nature, a meeting with someone, the sacramental gesture. To pray with such images is an excellent apprenticeship for meditation. Everything should lead us to God by a relation-ship-through-sight. "Let us look at him who looks at us" said St. Teresa of Avila. But as often as possible we must practice interiorizing what we see. In this area one can reach some quite surprising results. Contemplated in this way the faces of our brothers and sisters can become icons for us, disfigured ones perhaps, but our inner light can transfigure them.

Family prayer

This too is making a comeback. I know of one family that was transformed after having begun night prayer again on weekends: parents and children from sixteen to twenty-two. They consider it important for the younger children. "If our child," says Cecile, "comes to realize that prayer is part of her parents' life, a seed is sown which may grow in her." And another mother says: "We don't tell our children to say their prayers; we tell them that we are going to try to pray with them; there should be no authoritarian approach when dealing with prayer." The following is rarer, but so very suggestive: "In the morning we make half an hour's meditation in silence. The children know about it; they come, sometimes one, sometimes the other, sometimes none of them at all, to spend a few minutes with us. It is important that they should see us praying."

I have also noticed that more and more frequently people ask me to lead a prayer before meals. One of the great obstacles to family prayer, from the prayer of the young couple to the big night prayer grouping parents and children, seems to be fear: a fear made up of much bashfulness, a bit of human respect, and the desire not to make it a burden. But sometimes remarkable things can happen. A nineteen-year-old girl told me: "I think that my parents are believers, but they never pray!" That was not true; but in that family each member led a very individualistic prayer life.

How to set up a "prayer corner"

Nowadays, people everywhere are setting up "prayer corners." In a church that is too large; for a group or community; in an apartment. How does one go about this?

— Keep *silence* in mind.

The ideal: a little anteroom, making a barrier against unwanted noises (conversations in the corridor; radio or TV). If this is not possible, try having a double door providing an air-cushion. Put up a picture, serious or smiling, to remind those who pass here or who live nearby that they can give you a great gift: silence.

— *Start with a place or a corner that is absolutely empty.*

This is how, at Taizè, they managed to create a prayer corner in the little romanesque church. It was a rather ugly junk room. Disregarding the displeasure of the people who used it as such, it was entirely emptied, and the beauty of its architectural lines reappeared. Then, very discreetly, it was furnished and decorated. I remember especially the lovely icons, and the indirect lighting. Everybody loves to go and pray there now.

Avoid total emptiness (gives a cold impression), but have only a few things, and rather big ones, so as to avoid the impression of clutter. Harmonize the styles, the masses, the lines and colors. The best I have seen combine maroon and beige with a little yellow and white. That makes a beautiful and restful impression.

Carefully study the lighting; make it as indirect as possible. Have enough light so that one can read; but keep it subdued.

If there is a tabernacle, let it be simple but really artistic. Avoid all showy artisanship and vulgar originality. Use all the money available here.

Seating: Think of people of different ages, and those with rheumatism. Not everybody indulges in yoga. Put benches against the walls, so one can lean on these. On the carpet, small benches and cushions (very firm ones) for those who want to try Zen.

Not too many house plants or flowers. A Japanese bouquet, a rose in a crystal vase, a few dahlias; or again stemless flowers in a plate: gentians or water lilies.

Continual prayer

Smile if you like, but I am going to relate to you my discoveries about "ejaculatory prayers." This is the name given to short prayers fired up to God at any moment of the day, in the midst of any task or worry. One of my interviews brought me to a committed Catholic who happens to be a government official. I was taken aback by his reaction to my question: "How do you pray?" An embarrassed silence followed; then he said: "I don't pray; I don't pray any more." I stopped the tape recorder and we discussed this for a moment, "You, a well-known believer, a practicing Catholic, you say you don't pray any more?" All of a sudden he said: "I can't get along without God." Then he explained to me that he has, in fact, given up the prayers he used to say, at fixed times, using stereotyped formulas. But, he added, during the day I constantly glance up to God: at a moment of joy (particularly before the beauty of a landscape or a meeting with a noble character) or in difficult moments, when a serious decision has to be taken, when there is some sorrow to be borne. "And this I do," he added, "simply to strengthen my union with God, to remain in touch with him."

Not only did I find ejaculatory prayers in vogue again, but there is today a whole movement towards continual prayer, a search for union with God more or less diffuse and confused, but very real. This union is reinforced especially by using the beautiful ejaculation: "Lord, help me!" and also by words of thanks and admiration: "Be you blessed!" This kind of continual prayer is a sort of benediction of life and of the world, an unceasing dialogue with the Creator and Savior. Prayer in the usual sense remains an important moment in the life of a believer, but it also gives, in a wider sense, a sort of background to his entire life, a life of union with God.

Oriental meditations

Some friends of mine, a couple in their sixties, told me that they had signed up for a spiritual weekend. They proceeded to the designated room, opened the door, and saw about twenty people lying on their backs. They retreated in haste, saying, "Excuse us; we must have gotten the wrong door." But the priest in charge came and met them. "You are here for the spiritual weekend? This is the right place. Come in, and lie down." Results? Let me sum up what they had to say.

With the help of some precise advice they managed to relax more than they had ever done before. They put aside everything they had been ruminating about. But they remained in contact with those who, like them, breathed together very slowly. "The breath of God; the breath of life!" Then "we got up and sat on chairs. The younger ones, and those most accustomed to the procedure, sat on the carpet, legs crossed under them. Then, again guided by the leader, we entered, little by little, into a prayer of interior silence. We seemed to have found our way to a deep zone of our being. We were totally present to God at last."

Thus, some Christians have discovered a mingling of Christian prayer with oriental techniques. Others, though, react quite violently against this invasion which they consider dangerous: yoga, Zen, Transcendental Meditation.

I think it is unfortunate that the ones who oppose all this act out of a certain surliness (or fear?) which makes them refuse to dialogue, and in some cases, condemn without always knowing what is really in question. No doubt, some discernment is needed, but it should be clear sighted and well meaning. We can at least begin with one obvious fact, on which we shall have much more to say later, and which makes any actual effort to pray something to be sympathized with: for all of us, the main thing is the desire for union with God.

Here is one original aspect of this oriental invasion. It

poses the preliminary question: "Who is praying?" Generally, the candidate for prayer hurries on to two other questions: "Which God am I going to pray to?" (This is the question of an intelligent faith), and "What kind of prayer?" (This is the question about forms and methods). But in doing so one runs the risk of not paying enough attention to the condition of the one who is praying. Is he phlegmatic? Nervous? With thoughts and sentiments scattered everywhere? Superficial? Worried? In all such cases Yoga, Zen or even this or that, borrowed from the wisdom of the Far East, offer us something to bridle our anarchical minds, something to make flexible a stiffened body, so as to attain peace and depth. It is the discovery of the body, with its attitudes, relaxation and respiration; and of mental silence. Do we really need to go so far to look for this? In fact, there did seem to be a lack in this area. One may call it spiritual luxury, snobbery, mental hallucinogens . . . perhaps. But one can also find there a precious help to live one's daily life, and to devote oneself to prayer.

An experience of mine influenced me deeply: three years of Transcendental Meditation. I had been advised to try it for reasons of mental health, as a way of relaxing. I think it did help me to get back to normal. But to what extent? At that particular time, mental prayer and true family living also brought me joy and peace. I cannot tell which did what.

But I can say something about the dangers. Narcissism, selfishness. One is too taken up with oneself; one keeps looking for results; and one tends to adopt a "don't give a hoot" attitude towards everything else. At least, that was what happened to me. But I think that for many others this same tendency occurs. This physical and mental hygiene makes one too self-centered.

The second danger is this: you have to find twenty minutes each morning and evening. It's so agreeable (stretched out in an easy chair, while carefully avoiding any kind of effort), and I got so attached to it that sometimes I sacrificed my mental prayer time. I did manage to hang on to my beloved mental prayer, so that I was able to resist in time, but I think that these oriental methods, when presented to Christians as a complement to their life of faith and love, end up by taking over completely; one has no time or inclination left for anything else.

Third danger: gliding off towards worlds which separate us from our Christian faith. True, I was repeatedly told that Transcendental Meditation was not something "religious" and could adapt itself to any sort of faith; but after all these lessons and sessions you finally breathe an air of Hinduism, and (how shall I express it?) one comes

---

Buddhist prayer

The temple is located on the high,
difficult hill.
The path is full of pitfalls,
and surrounded by serpents.
The wind is cold and biting;
and the sky somber.
It is a struggle one must begin over and over again,
lighting a lamp in the temple.
My own lamp has blown out;
I relight and relight it over and over.
What a joy to light the lamp in the temple
to guide the faithful old people back up to the sanctuary.
May my life be like the lamp of the temple,
and guide faltering steps towards the gates of Nirvana,
the eternal truth.

Poem of Matsuko, Buddhist religious

---

to have complete confidence in a simple technique, which might make one believe that salvation lies in that, and not in Christ. It was mainly for this reason that I gave it up.

I should be less categorical speaking of Yoga and Zen, which are at once less overpowering and more demanding. I think one can limit oneself to the mere technique of the postures, of respiration and of hygiene in Yoga, and to the simple seated posture (the wonderful erectness of the spinal column!) in Zen, and its different expressions, such as the art of flower arrangement and the simple and peace-inducing nobility of the gestures. But there is a price to be paid: one has to be serious and persevering, and not expect great results immediately at a slight cost in efforts.

Conclusion: we should not systematically fear what can be helpful, but we must look out for side effects. The best test to evaluate these things is to verify whether by using these methods we really enter more deeply into our own Christian experience.

Lectio divina *(spiritual reading)*

I put in the Latin name, because after our quick trip to India and Japan we shall now go back to our own medieval past, by considering a currently popular but very ancient form of prayer: the meditation of the Bible, and in general, spiritual reading.

It is a difficult type of prayer, precisely because it seems so easy; one can be fooled by this. One starts off intending to pray, and one finds oneself enjoying the pleasure of study. That is why the name given to this prayer is so important: reading, yes; but divine reading, because it should be an encounter with God. It calls for a loving attention to God, and an eagerness to hear what he wishes to tell us in the passage considered.

The only effective way of turning a reading into a prayer, according to those who have chosen this method of praying, is to read slowly, and to make pauses. In her very practical book *Too Deep For Words,* Thelma Hall advises various ways of proceeding:

— A meditated reading. As soon as you feel yourself touched by a phrase, stop reading and repeat it several times so as to cut down on your reflective activity and to promote the grasp of the idea by the heart. For instance, if you repeat to yourself "if anyone thirsts, let him come to me and drink," or even, more simply, "to me, to me" you are making meditation, not with your intellect, but by using the universal method of repetition.

If God gives you the gift of silence, then stop repeating and hold yourself simply before him in an attention full of love, prolonging this inner attitude which the words you meditated on and repeated have created in you. "Yes, I thirst; Lord, I am coming to you!"

Of course, distractions will come. When you notice them start your reading again, and stop as soon as a new passage moves you.

— Reading with active interiorization. Get help from a good commentary, and think about the passage by asking questions like: "What does this passage tell me? What is God trying to tell me?"

When God's word speaks to you interiorly, let it descend to the depths of your being to seize you, to purify you, enlighten you and encourage you. Stop eating and give yourself time to digest! Remain in silence, offering yourself with all sincerity to the word which is acting in you and transforming you.

Personally, I prefer what I call the "gospel encounter." This is a reading of the gospel with a certain change in perspective. Instead of going to meet Jesus in Palestine by leaving aside my daily life, I try to bring Jesus into that life. The real Jesus, of course, the Jesus who lived in Palestine such as we find him in every passage of the gospel; but especially — and this is the special twist I give to this encounter — Jesus risen again, who is fully living, and who is looking at me and at what I am doing at this moment. "Let Christ keep his eye on you."

His glance demands that I make the most of my life, for Christ wants to bring about through me what he obviously could not bring about in Palestine, two thousand years ago. I can be for him an "extra humanity." I must live evangelically in my work, my relationships, my worries bravely borne. The gospel encounter is the meeting of my life with the spirit of Jesus Christ. "In this situation, with so and so, how would he react?"

Pilgrimages

Coming back from Quebec a priest spoke to me with enthusiasm of a place of pilgrimage, the sanctuary of Beauvoir. "The Assumptionists, who are in charge there," he told me, "have set up in the forest a large way of the cross, with life-sized statues at each station. To the pilgrims who want to hear they comment on these scenes; it is a catechism lesson for people many of whom never go to church any more."

Much the same thing could be said about what the priests at Ars do, and the Jesuits at La Louvesc. Discovering a sanctuary and a saint has often transformed a simple tourist into a deeply moved man, who learns how to pray again. No crowd is as variegated as that found at Lourdes. A pilgrimage is really a grace offered to everyone.

You win that grace by using your feet, not to mention all the fatigues and sometimes the privations that the journey entails. In the old days, the great pilgrimages called for great endurance, and many died on the way. Without hope, such rashness would have been a sort of suicide, but there was so much faith and love in the pilgrims that for a long time, going on a pilgrimage was considered on a par with the sacrament of reconciliation. People started off intending to ask forgiveness for some act of hatred or some other crime. At all events, today as yesterday, the high point of the pilgrimage is confession and communion, combined with devotion to the Most Blessed Virgin and the saints.

On a recent pilgrimage I made, I strongly felt this

symbolism of our march. Our feet and our hearts were plodding ahead; in our collective silence and in the moments of prayer we were really going towards God; the movement itself was a prayer. "Lord," says St. Augustine, "although you go nowhere, still it is only with great difficulty that we come back to you" (*Confessions* 8:3).

II.
JESUS TEACHES US HOW TO PRAY

We are constantly scrutinizing Jesus Christ as the teacher and model of fraternal charity, and that's very good. Yet we search less deeply into his teachings on prayer, seeking instead for gurus when our guru is right there before us.

Everything that Jesus does and says is a revelation in the strongest sense of the term. And so his prayer is a part of Revelation, it is by watching him pray that we discover that he is *the Son*. And he wants us to develop within us a truly filial prayer.

But since prayer consists in an effort toward union, did Jesus need to make this effort? Is he not always united to the Father? It is precisely there that we see the necessity of prayer: the closest union will always demand explicit prayer

---

The most common Jewish prayer: Shema Israel

Hear, O Israel! The Lord is our God, the Lord alone! Therefore you shall love the Lord, your God, with all your heart, and with all your soul, and with all your strength. Take to heart these words which I enjoin on you today. Drill them into your children. Speak of them at home and abroad, whether you are busy or at rest. Bind them at your wrist as a sign and let them be as a pendant on your forehead. Write them on the doorposts of your houses and on your gates. (Dt 6:4-9)

---

of us at certain times. Objections against prayer are meaningless in the presence of Jesus at prayer. Since he himself prayed, we too can and must pray.

"Then he went out to the mountain to pray, spending the night in communion with God" (Lk 6:12). There is no more powerful call to prayer than this.

Jesus' Jewish prayer

Meditation on Jesus Christ's prayer allows us to know his Jewish heritage better and to reflect upon it. He knew the *Shema Israel* and recited it morning and night, the prayer of the ninth hour (three o'clock in the afternoon, Acts 3:1), the prayer at meals and frequent bursts of praise. He went to the synagogue to pray, to the Temple during his pilgrimages to Jerusalem. He noticed how prayer had deteriorated through ostentation, routine, and bargaining with God: "If I say these prayers, I shall have a right to this or that." We sense his standards for prayer in his often very harsh remarks on prayer that is babbling, self-interested, and formalistic.

He clearly loved the psalms, and through them we can learn something about his heart. He entered into these sentiments. When we pray the psalms we are close to him, we are in him. This is a powerful caution not to seek here, there and everywhere for models of prayer when we already have this treasure that can fashion us as it fashioned Christ.

Jesus' prayer in the gospel

Jesus did not pray simply like any good Jew. His prayer reveals to us an absolutely unique relationship with the Father and hence the filial overtones that must characterize Christian prayer.

Jesus' prayer is first of all a prayer of exultation, as it has been transmitted to us by Matthew and Luke:

"At that moment Jesus rejoiced in the Holy Spirit and said: 'I offer you praise, O Father, Lord of heaven and

earth, because what you have hidden from the learned and the clever you have revealed to the merest children. Yes, Father, you have graciously willed it so' " (Lk 10:21).

One man lived on this earth who was able to call God "Father" with pure joy and loving admiration, exactly as God had willed in creating the human race. Every prayer must first of all be praise such as this in order to reach God in the very wake of Jesus' prayer. Petitions and combats will come later, but Christian prayer must never remain too far from loving and joyous peace: *"I praise you."* This is an infallible test of the presence of the Spirit without which there is neither the desire to pray nor authentic prayer: *"Jesus rejoiced in the Holy Spirit and said: 'I offer you praise, O Father . . . ' "* (Lk 10:21).

This is one of those chains of thought in the gospel that we must not take in a distracted way. Otherwise we will hear it a thousand times and repeat that without the Spirit it is useless to want to pray, meanwhile continuing to seek prayer far from the Spirit and, disastrously, far from the model sketched here in four decisive characteristics:

Joy *(he rejoiced)*

The impulsion of the Spirit *(in the Spirit)*

Filial enthusiasm *(Father)*

Praise *(I praise you).*

That is really the launching pad of our life of prayer, and to discover it in contemplation Jesus is an incomparable guarantee. There are a thousand paths to prayer but only one guide: Christ and his way of saying "Father." In the last analysis we could sum up all prayer as the way of pronouncing "Father" like Jesus.

His joyful enthusiasm is the sign of something that introduces us into the innermost depths of prayer. It is a continuous cleaving to God: *"In the beginning was the Word; the Word was turned toward God."* It is not enough to translate "in God's presence" or "with God." The text indicates a "movement toward," an orientation.

As man, Jesus enters into this movement of the Word, of the Son. The essence of prayer is this first and last attitude that best expresses what we are. To use the words of St. Augustine: "You made us turned toward you, a movement toward you." We disfigure prayer when it becomes an obligation, a forced labor, a bargaining. By nature it is the most joyous and the most selfless movement because it is what makes us what we are: we are prayer by the very fact that we exist. The glory of explicit prayer is that it makes us become aware of our fundamental being: we are sons and daughters who must live like sons and daughters, and that is a good thing! *"Father, I praise you."*

A second face of Jesus' prayer: intercession. We can intuit it throughout the gospel, and sometimes it finds explicit expression: *"Simon . . . I have prayed for you"* (Lk 22:31-32). When we read this, how our desire wells up! "Lord, pray for me."

The entire Chapter 17 of St. John reveals to us Jesus' prayer for his disciples. Granted, it is not a verbatim record of his prayer, but under the Spirit's inspiration John tells us how Christ thinks of us and what he asks for us.

At the moment it was pronounced, it asked for the coming fruits of the sacrifice of the Cross, soon to be fulfilled. Now it is the prayer of the risen Christ, interceding for us at the right hand of the Father: *"Therefore he is able to save those who approach God through him, since he forever lives to make intercession for them"* (Hb 7:25).

I don't think we are much inclined to contemplate Christ in this way in his mysterious exultation. We look at him on the roads of Galilee and on the Cross. And yet we must — and it is the great benefit of Chapter 17 — enter into these words that also give us the tone of the glorious Jesus praying for his Church. Jesus' two faces (the face of yesterday and the face of today) will appear constantly as superimposed on one another:

— Father, I have glorified you *on earth.*

— Glorify me *at your side.*

Two great petitions have sprung and therefore still spring up at the very moments we come face to face with Jesus:

—*"Father, that they may know you and that they may know me."*

—*"That all may be one."*

What a grace to be able to be so sure of Christ's thoughts. We are snatched from our habitual, often constricted requests, we enter into God's magnificent intentions for humankind.

And first of all to give all men and women eternal joy, eternal life. In other words, to know God and to know Jesus Christ. The same knowledge. Jesus must make the Father known by making the Son known. He specifies that this is indeed "his work," his mission: to reveal the Name, the name that is "Love." Jesus' greatest suffering was to run afoul of the rejections of this knowledge: the best educated Jews, and often the holiest among them, have not accepted that God should be Love as Jesus revealed him to be. His last prayer on earth and his prayer in heaven now is the prayer of the great mission: *"That they may know you!"*

Even when we know God and his love, life "in the world" will always remain perilous. If anyone ever understood the exact scope of these dangers, it was certainly Jesus. In his prayer, joy and concern are intermingled: *"I come to you, O Father . . . but these are in the world: . . . guard them from the evil one!"* (Jn 17:11; 15).

The pathetic cry "guard them!" has sometimes been seen as an invitation to form refugee-communities. Fear of the world, flight from the world have been preached. But Jesus speaks clearly: *"I do not ask you to take them out of the world. . . . I have sent them into the world"* (Jn 17:15; 18). There is need of communitarian fervors and securities, but they are intended to fashion courageous missionaries.

True communitarian cohesion, that is to say, fraternal love, is for Jesus the best missionary advertisement: *"That all may be one . . . that the world may believe"* (Jn 17:21). A Christian community (and the entire Church) can only export what it produces, it proclaims love when it is love. "Let them be united if they want to talk to us of love!"

That was the great cry that launched the ecumenical movements, an extension of Jesus' prayer, *"That they may be one!"*

The unbelievable thing is the model of unity that he proposes to us by asking his Father on our behalf:

"That all may be one as you, Father, are in me, and I in you; . . . that they may be one as we are one — I living in them, you living in me — that their unity may be complete" (Jn 17:21-23).

If we dared, we would say to Jesus: "Come now, you are dreaming! You who know people so well, through your bruised flesh and heart, how can you actually see them capable of attaining perfect unity?"

But who am I to set limits to Jesus' prayer? If I am skeptical of his grandiose perspectives I turn away from him, I sit on the side of the road, I no longer am among those to whom he can say: *"Come, follow me!"*

He wants to lead us along a long road of humanity. This humanity has a long history, O ancient pithecanthropic brothers! It will emerge into the extraordinary when God will be all in all (cf. 1 Cor 15:28), and that will be perfect unity! In the midst (at the start?) of this adventure Jesus sees far ahead. He was never afraid of modest beginnings: the mustard seed becomes a tree for all the birds of the sky (cf. Mt 13:31). To follow Jesus is to dream with him of the immense hopes that make us grow to his stature: *"Father, that they may be one like us!"* When I enter into his prayer, I hope like him, and that is not a petty hope.

Many things are said, in few but rich words. First, this "like us" that shakes our timidities: "Dare to look at the model!" Jesus' behavior reveals that between the Father and himself, through the Spirit, unity is not a juxtaposition, a coexistence, but the dynamics of love. Father, Son and Holy Spirit know one another (that means something inexhaustible when it refers to God), and each one plays his own role in the great common works: creation, redemption, sanctification.

Since Jesus himself urges us to go toward this model of

32

Praying with the missal

Now that excellent Sunday and daily missals are available, it would be a pity not to make greater use of all the wealth the missal contains.

I shall give but one example: the first prayer of the Mass which used to be called the "Collect," and now is called the "Opening Prayer." Not all of them are works of genius, but many are true masterpieces. It is a real religious literary genre, characterized by its structure and its density of meaning. Here is an especially rich one: the Opening Prayer for the Mass for the evangelization of peoples.

Lord, you willed to make of your Church the sign of the salvation which you have brought to the world, so that the work of the Savior might be continued until the end of time. Revive the ardor of your faithful, make them understand that they are called to labor for the salvation of all people, so that all humanity may become the one people of your children, ever more united, ever more numerous. This we ask through Jesus Christ your Son our Lord and God, who with you and the Holy Spirit reigns now and forever, Amen.

This same format, very carefully crafted, is found in most of these models of prayer:

1. First, the contemplation of what God is, of what he wills and brings about: "You willed to make of your Church the sign of the salvation which you brought to the world." ˙

2. The childlike request: "Revive the ardor of your faithful."

3. Recourse to Christ, which characterizes Christian prayer and culminates in trinitarian adoration: "Through Jesus Christ, with you and the Holy Spirit."

unity-love (*That they may be one* like *us*), perhaps we can go so far as to imagine their reciprocal contemplation, for that is also what unites. The happiness to see in others only beauty and gift, admiration that never ceases nurturing love.

Alas! We start diminishing it right away. Can we admire our brothers and sisters totally and tirelessly? No, but we can reverse the proportion between criticism and admiration by becoming stronger in the art of admiring, by our will to admire. It is said that love is blind. Actually, the eyes of love detect only the best and can't see the faults of the beloved very well. So much gained for union! To think of Jesus' gaze at the Father and the Father's gaze at Jesus will help us to look at one another "like them."

We must decidedly multiply our boldness: *"Father, that they may be one* in *us."* That is Jesus' prayer. Our fraternal efforts are divine, they introduce us to the exchanges of trinitarian love. Saint John's golden text tells us that there is only one love:

> *As the Father has loved me,*
> *So I have loved you.*
> *You will live in my love*
> *By loving one another*
> *As I have loved you.*

Here again we have the "as," but linked with another Johannine word that is just as important: "live." Love gives us a dwelling place in God, and God also lives in us: it is the indwelling, the secret of unity. Our fraternal action unites us among ourselves "as" the Father and the Son are united, and "in" the Father and the Son. Jesus' extraordinary request *"that their unity may be complete,"* should not discourage or delude us. We can go forward on these paths but only through the Spirit who makes us dwell in God. A love is given to us but we must live it: *"he who abides in love abides in God, and God in him"* (1 Jn 4:16). Those who are called to unity are those who reveal God by their passion for unity wherever they live in groups:

"So shall the world know that you sent me and that you loved them as you loved me" (Jn 17:23).

Can this great prayer of Christ become our very own? In its original form, no. It is truly Christ's prayer. But it can make us the kind of men and women of prayer that the Father wants: adorers, certainly, and also petitioners. When we raise up to him John's three great petitions *"That they may know you; Guard them from the evil one; That they may be one"* (Jn 17) we enter into Christ's own tone and draw out of ourselves. We open our thoughts to the Church, to missionaries, to unity, to all those who fight the powers of darkness. That is petition uttered loud and clear.

The third face of Jesus' prayer: anguish. *"Father . . . take this cup from me; yet not my will but yours be done"* (Lk 22:42).

First came the imperious burst *(Glorify me; That they may share my joy; I want them to be with me)*, and now follows the exhausted and hesitant groan. And yet this is precisely where Jesus is our model in a special way. We shall never have any better words than his.

It is one thing to think of God and to treat him courteously, it is quite another to cry out our distress to him savagely. One day, someone asked me if when we addressed God we had the right to weep. Yes, we have the right to weep and cry out, to drag our distress up close to the prostrate Christ: *"he offered prayers and supplications with loud cries and tears to God"* (Hb 5:7).

Prayer is all the more authentic when we encounter God person to person. Think of the many distracted and formalistic prayers that are said, and then come back to Gethsemane. We are not distracted when we say: I can't take any more; I'm afraid, save me. If Christ had not passed through all that, could we really say that he had prayed?

Words we should keep carefully in our hearts illumine his road of anguish. The Father had said to him: *"You are my beloved Son."* He remained in this sunlight for a long time until the hour when he cried out: *"My God, why have you forsaken me?"* But he did say *"my God"* and *"Father, into your hands I commend my spirit!"* A prayer of anguish that ceased to cling to God through lack of trust would be perdition, and it is at Gethsemane that we see this battle being fought between anguish and trust. For the first time a distance was visible between the Father's will and Jesus' will. He who had said *"I do always what pleases him, his will is my food"* remained for a moment blocked by fear. Who will guess how long he was able to repeat only *"Take this cup from me,"* realizing full well that it was his own will? How can we fail to thank him for having gone to the very depths of our fears, of our crazed desires to escape what is crushing us, by showing us the course to follow, the course he followed: *"No! Not my will."*

By repeating the account of this combat three times, the gospel instills a vital conviction in us: we must succeed in making trust gain the upper hand. "Not my will but yours, because I know it is a loving will and that you will help me." To believe this at such a moment is the greatest victory of prayer, it helps us to remain in the embrace of an incomprehensible love. "You are powerful, you love me, and I shall die in a horrible way, but I put my trust in you." Thousands of believers have been able to say similar things because there has been a Gethsemane.

"Teach us to pray"

Jesus has already taught us to pray by revealing his own prayer to us, but he also gives us lessons on how to pray in a very direct way.

First of all, and we have just seen how Jesus himself lives what he teaches, there can be no petition without trust. Christian prayer is a prayer certain of being granted, as a famous verse in the Gospel of Mark affirms: *"I give you my word, if you are ready to believe that you will receive whatever you ask for in prayer, it shall be done for you"* (Mk 11:24).

At this point, there are those who smile or utter a sigh. That's not true! We have prayed so hard without being heard. Discussions on this answer to prayer are many, and we shall have to talk about them again. For the moment we listen to our teacher of prayer, and his teaching is clear: "Believe!" Place yourself immediately in this act of believing and remain in it, otherwise your prayer will not be serious.

Jesus himself lived this "Believe!" We know it from Saint John's words (cf. Jn 11:41-42). Jesus is preparing to raise Lazarus from the dead, and he prays publicly: *"Father, I thank you for having heard me."* He is giving thanks for being heard even before it happens. He adds: *"I know that you always hear me."*

To petition with such complete assurance is so far from our own ways of praying that we are tempted to think: "Obviously, that's Jesus!" But that must be our way of praying as well. For it is to us that Jesus says: *"Believe that you will be heard, that you have already been heard."* It is the same lesson of faith when the petition is made directly to him. He shakes the epileptic's father who taunted him with an "if you can" in the manner of our habitual half-hopeful half-skeptical petitions. *"If you can? Everything is possible to a man who trusts"* (Mk 9:23). Then the father cries out a solid *"I believe!"* But he immediately understands its limitations. *"No, I don't believe enough, help me to have greater faith."*

Jesus also takes the measure of this modest faith and he finds it sufficient, since he can heal the child.

The whole question, and it is not an easy one, is to know when our "lack of faith" still has some power over God. Perhaps when it is a sincere desire to have precisely a faith that could move our mountains. A faith such as this is far from us. But we want it, we fight against doubt, we have real experiences of trust that make us advance. We believe Jesus when he tells us: "Your prayer is already answered." To pray is "already" a grace, trying to have faith is such a great moment (Father, I know you always hear me) that the granting of the prayer begins. If we remain in the dark but with the will to believe that God is working, we shall some day see the power of our prayer: it makes us share in the power of salvation in which we shall never believe as wholeheartedly as we should.

Another attitude we need if we are to pray in a serious way is to want to do God's will. There, too, we must certainly make progress: "I want what you want, but increase my desire to want it." Anyone who prays without being deeply concerned with what God asks of everyone and asks him in an individualistic way would not be praying seriously.

Besides, there is no question of being arrogant in the face of this will. That would be outside of life's ways and very theoretical. "I have cancer? Very well, Lord . . . My little Mark is going to die? That's fine, Lord." No, that's not it at all.

What kind of prayer, then? As far as I can imagine it, since I have not trodden along those roads, prayer can only drag itself toward God's will, but it is turned in that direction: "Help me to live like that if you expect it of me, show me how to live amid this horror."

Jesus has fashioned a prayer for us. One short prayer — *"Do not multiply words!"* (Mt 6:7). But for all that we must still keep insisting and pounding at the door of God's heart (cf. Lk 18:1-8). This precious prayer, this Our Father chiseled with words that Jesus has chosen, is precisely the prayer of God's will. Apparently, the Our Father is composed of two parts, but actually the whole prayer is a petition revolving around the sun-petition: *"Your will be done."* And your Name will be hallowed, your Kingdom will come. But to keep us in your will, give us bread, keep us in your forgiveness, make us strong against temptation. That is the heart and the words of all those who pray seriously.

Praying to Jesus

Jesus who prays, and who teaches us to pray, is also the Jesus to whom we pray. The conclusions of the liturgical prayers provide us, on this point, with a number of very delicate variations.

When we pray to the Father we make Jesus the great intercessor the bearer of our desires: *"We ask this, O Father, through Jesus Christ your Son who reigns with you and the Holy Spirit."*

If we are praying to the Father, with mention of the Son, the latter's name reappears like this in the conclusion: *"Father, make us share in the divinity of your Son . . . who with you and the Holy Spirit lives and reigns."*

When we pray directly to Jesus we end in this way: *''O you who reign with the Father and the Holy Spirit."* But this is so rare that we might ask, since Jesus is the mediator between the Father and ourselves, whether we should not, in fact, pray through him rather than to him.

True enough. He is our mediator, but a very special mediator, a totally unique one. Other mediators are only intermediaries. A good mediator between A and B tries to understand both A and B in order to harmonize their views. But he is not A or B.

Evening prayer in the Orthodox liturgy

Joyous light of the holy glory of the immortal Father,
Celestial, holy, blessed Jesus Christ.
As we reach the setting of the sun and see the light of evening,
Let us celebrate God, Father, Son, and Holy Spirit.
You are worthy to be honored at all times, by holy voices,
O Son of God who gives life; wherefore the world glorifies you.

> *Phôs hilaron,* in Greek.
> Vesper hymn *Svete tikhi* in Slavonic.
> One of the Church's most ancient prayers
> (second century).

On the contrary, if Christ is the perfect mediator between God and man, it is because he *is* at once God and man. We can, therefore, sometimes pray to God through him our mediator, and sometimes pray to him, for he is our God. But in this latter case he remains our mediator because he is God only in so far as he is God's Son. The prayer we address to him is then doubly filial; he brings it up immediately towards the Father because he is always as we have said, "with the Father." And we are led to pray to him, the Son, so as to resemble him as sons.

The contrary is also true. When we pray "through Jesus Christ" we pray to him directly because if we realize what we are doing we believe in his divine power of mediation.

In no one else, either in Mary or in the saints, do we have such confidence as we have when we say. *"I ask you this, Father, through your Son Jesus Christ."*

This total confidence in Jesus goes back a long way, even to the very earliest days of the Church. Stoned to death, Stephen prayed: *"Lord Jesus, receive my spirit"* (Acts 7:59). He was saying in a striking manner that henceforth we could address Christ as God. He was not only our model to imitate, but the Almighty One to be implored.

Here we could begin a whole treatise based on the gospel about learning how to pray to Christ. Obviously, it is a matter of faith, the kind which elicited the admiration of Jesus himself. *"I have not found such great faith even in Israel"* (Mt 8:10). By this exclamation Jesus reveals to us something about God and about prayer. We must not pray with just any sort of confidence; it must be, as he said, literally an "admirable" faith. Consider the following six supplicants who are obviously given to us as models: the leper (Mt 8:1-4); the centurion (Mt 8:5-10); the two blind men (Mt 9:27-31); the father of the epileptic boy (Mk 9:14-29); the Canaanite woman (Mt 15:21-28); and the good thief (Lk 23:43).

It always comes back to faith. *"Woman, great is your faith!"* Prayer is the daughter of faith, the school of faith, the mother of the finest acts of faith. The best methods of prayer are not worth these two essential counsels: "Verify your faith; and then put some muscle into your faith." We would really be able to pray to Jesus if we had the power of faith that the leper had; *"Lord, if you will, you can make me clean."* Just thinking about this jolts us back to our own flabby requests.

Flabby, because they lack faith in the power of God, but also in his compassion, one of the great revelations Jesus brought us. These six supplicants are in fact driven to Jesus by their distress; and he is moved thereby "down to his entrails" to use the Biblical term which so vividly expresses God's compassion.

Since Moses' time, we knew that God is not an unmoved spectator. *"I have seen the distress of my people; I have heard their cries, and I have come down to deliver them"* (Ex 3:7-8). He came down in Jesus Christ; and the gospel so often shows him "moved to his entrails" so that our prayer in our distress can often be limited to telling him, "You see, don't you?" On one condition, which we must always repeat: that our "You See?" should reflect a faith which allows us and even enables us to measure (O mystery!) the action of the Lord. *"Let it be done to you as you have believed"* (Mt 8:13).

What kind of faith? We know who Jesus is; these petitioners did not. All the more reason for us to pray to him with immense faith; but the example of these six remains very important, especially in our days, when with all the confused arguments about miracles, we no longer believe in the power of Jesus Christ. The result is plain. From our unbelieving distress nothing can arise but a feeble prayer which measures parsimoniously what Christ might be able to do for us. *"Let it be done to you according to your faith!"* is a frightening word; a word of hope or of condemnation which judges not Christ, but ourselves.

Praying in Jesus

It would seem that we have considered all that we should as regards Christ and our prayer. He is its model and teacher, its mediator before God, and the one who listens to our prayer when we pray to him directly. Yet there is a final step to take, a step towards interiorizing our prayer. In all we have seen up to now Jesus remained on the outside. But two characteristic expressions, "in Christ" and "in his name" bring him into the interior of our prayer itself.

With the Risen Christ a new prayer will arise. He told us this when saying farewell. *"Until now you have not asked anything in my name"* (Jn 16:24). What is this prayer "in his name"?

It is much more than a mere formula: "Father, in Jesus' name, I ask you. . . ." which would still leave us apart from Christ. In the Bible, the name means the person who is communicated. To act in Jesus' name, to pray in Jesus' name, means to penetrate into his life of relationships, and to make our prayer part of his prayer.

Here we have one of the results of the mystery of our incorporation into Christ. We are not apart from the Risen Christ; with him we make up a body (the mystical Body), but we need to live this reality, mysterious as it is, as consciously as we can. This means that we are invited to enter into the current of love that unites him to the Father by the Spirit. This was his supreme desire. *"That your love for me may live in them, and I may live in them"* (Jn 17:26).

This shows us how deeply we are brought into intimate union with him. The important thing is not to hunt for ideas, sentiments, modes of behavior, but for union: he in us, and we in him. This is a long way from using his name in a vainglorious and rather external way which might bring us to brandish it like a sort of campaign pennant: "We are Christ's party!" If we did, we would risk a severe condemnation. *"None of those who cry out, 'Lord, Lord,' will enter the Kingdom of God, but only the one who does the will of my Father in heaven. When that day comes, many will plead with me, 'Lord, Lord, have we not prophesied in your name? Have we not exorcised demons by its power? Did we not do many miracles in your name as well?' Then I will declare to them solemnly, 'I never knew you!'* " (Mt 7:21-23).

Of course, this does not condemn the desire to belong to Jesus' party, nor to call him Lord; but it puts us on guard against a superficial manner of making use of his name. We must merit to receive him very interiorly; and this implies two things: first, conforming ourselves as much as we can with the Father's will and making up our minds to behave like sons. And then, in the second place, making Christ's filial views our own, something we can do only in the depths of our souls. Then we shall receive his name, that is, his filial attitude. Our prayer "in his name," our prayer with him and in him then becomes a filial prayer. It's all included in the word "Father," provided that our life does not give the lie to this cry of love.

Prayer and the Holy Spirit

It is not all that easy to say "Father," and say it right. St. Paul points this out to us; we need the Holy Spirit.

"All who are led by the Spirit of God are sons of God. You did not receive a spirit of slavery leading you back into fear, but a Spirit of adoption through which we cry out, 'Abba!' (that is, 'Father!'). The Spirit himself gives witness with our spirit that we are children of God" (Rom 8:14-16).

Every prayer is an implicit request to the Spirit to change our mentality; we shall try for a moment to tear ourselves away from our ordinary heaviness, to rise to those lofty levels where the Spirit leads us.

He makes us say "Father" the way one falls in love. For an instant, at least, we are sure of being loved. How our lives would be transformed if we remained in that certainty! When a prayer finds and reinforces this certainty then one can say he has really prayed, that the Holy Spirit

43

really opened his lips. This is what St. Paul also tells us in the inexhaustible Chapter 8, verse 26. *"For we do not know how to pray as we ought; but the Spirit himself makes intercession for us with groanings which cannot be expressed in speech."* The Holy Spirit prays for us, in us, with us. How shall I put it? It is still our prayer, but enriched at its roots, and blossoming forth in the dimensions and hues of sonship, thus becoming Christ's own prayer in us, which every prayer should be. But, we must repeat it, this is possible only "in" the Spirit. To say that we go to the Father through Jesus Christ in the Holy Spirit is perfectly correct, and vital. Unfortunately, this still remains just a formula which does not make anything come to life, until we have decided to transform our prayers into experiences of the Spirit.

And these (too bad if I repeat myself) are experiences of sonship. This is the first component of the climate of prayer in the Spirit; in every way possible, it cries out "Father!"

The second component is openness to our brothers and sisters. It is not useless to keep saying this over and over. Mental prayer, petitionary prayer and Mass itself do not always (alas!) make us automatically more open to others. (Petitionary prayer often closes us in upon ourselves.) The fact that pious people are often suspected of selfishness is like an amber light flashing. The danger is that we might think of prayer as "a raising of our minds towards God" where we could soar off far from all concern about our brothers and sisters. But that prayer would go without the Spirit. He wants to see us grouped together; he untiringly builds up communities.

"For by him we have access in one Spirit to the Father. You are built upon the foundation of the apostles and prophets, Jesus Christ himself being the chief cornerstone. . . . In whom you also are built together into a habitation of God in the Spirit" (Ph 2:18-22).

Note the repeated use of "in." This is opposed to all the "outside of" which keep us away from true prayer, away from the Holy Spirit, away from the difficulties met with in our daily lives, away from the people we should support and help. Our prayer is truly prayer when it "includes all that," not a pious, unreal exercise, or an equally unreal twosome with "God alone." True prayer in the Spirit is recognized in that it is both a reaching out to others as well as to God. The more this irks us (not a terrible thing, since not everyone is naturally gregarious), the more we need to pray in the Spirit who will keep us open to others.

This openness will be characterized by a double effort: communion among ourselves, and concern about those who do not know Jesus. We know that we are praying in the Spirit when we remain at once community-minded and missionary-minded; when the mildness (or the sharpness) of our neighbor does not take up all our attention. Here is a last word from Jesus: *"You will receive power when the Holy Spirit comes down on you; then you are to be my witnesses"* (Acts 1:8). In fact, to go out to labor and to be a witness to Christ is so difficult that without the Holy Spirit we shall cave in first.

Another gift of the Holy Spirit to our prayer is improvisation. One day I was questioning a member of a senior citizen group on how they prayed during their meetings.

"Not much," he told me; "an Our Father and Hail Mary at the end."

And he added this, which struck me: "We do not know how to improvise prayers."

Where people do know how to improvise is in any charismatic group. Does this not hint at a connection between the Holy Spirit and spontaneous prayer? Who can, even in a group, be very personal, with a real song of the Spirit on his lips, and start a loving dialogue with God, or offer him vehement supplications? In prayer groups, and even in families this spontaneous prayer shows all the characteristics of real life: unexpected, it reveals the Spirit; it is often awkward, but humble, modest and very touching.

Such occasions impress those present. But watch out if it becomes too wordy, or which is worse, turns into exhibitionism.

Spontaneous collective prayer is indeed a sort of challenge. We must manage an improvisation that is at once personal and communal; we must speak directly to God, and also for the brothers and sisters who are listening. They will then be brought closer to God, or be irritated and embarrassed. More than ever, this kind of prayer must spring from the depths of the soul of the one praying, and speak to the depths of the souls of the others. It is truly an experience of the Spirit.

Liturgical prayer, the prayer of the Body of Christ

Our relationship with God certainly depends on the very special attention he pays to us, but this interest reaches us in the groups to which we belong, and hence in the Church. These two truths, God is for me, and God is for everybody else, are found, obviously, in our prayer, which is a prayer "in secret" (Mt 6:6) and also in liturgical prayer which is a prayer of the Church, and in the Church.

Paul's two exclamations are very striking. *"[He] loved me and gave himself for me"* (Gal 2:20); and *"Husbands, love your wives, as Christ loved the church. He gave himself up for her"* (Eph 5:25).

We find it difficult to live such a parallelism, and moreover, instead of speaking of parallelism we should talk of interpenetration, like the soloist with the choir. When discussing prayer some always say that they like to pray together, while others claim that they cannot pray save when alone. Here each one must keep an eye on himself if he wishes to maintain himself in true Christian equilibrium: habitual individual fervor must accompany strong participation in the major group efforts. The ones who participate best in the liturgy are the prayerful people to whom mental prayer has given a spiritual depth and substance. If their liking for mental prayer keeps them away from collective prayer, they should be on their guard. They risk losing the ecclesial sense, and even love; whoever is not a good companion in prayer will find it hard to be a true neighbor in daily life. It is surprising (and a great pity) that the Church has been obliged to make Mass obligatory. Older people remain obsessed with the question, "Is Mass still an obligation, yes or no?" One feels like asking them, "Yes or no, do you love this collective gathering with God?"

The liturgical prayer par excellence, the prayer of the Church, is obviously the Mass, but, as we have seen, a movement is taking shape towards the liturgical "Prayer of the Hours" (which among priests and religious is called "The Office"). Nor should we forget baptisms, marriages, funerals, penance services, which are more and more occasions for participation.

Still, certain "allergies" assume disturbing proportions. "Participating" (that's the key word) in gatherings of such heterogeneous groups which are often pretty cold, is the first and the greatest difficulty. Even among Christians, because of the locale and the pre-determined program, people hardly come out of their shells to exchange smiles, words, significant silences which would no doubt quickly transform these "strangers" into brothers and sisters. I think of the elderly lady who was upset by a young man at Mass; at the time that the "sign of peace" was to be exchanged he clasped her hand in a vise-like grip. "But sir," she exclaimed, "I do not know you."

One smiles at that, and yet have we ever seriously questioned ourselves on these frightening, water-tight attitudes which congeal our liturgies and turn off the young? The first step towards liturgical participation is something far different from sporadic efforts to show external signs of sympathy, which would lead us to selective friendliness. We need to get down to the mystery of this absolutely unique society, the Church, which is the Body of Christ.

When we speak of mystery, we speak of faith. It is from the depths of my faith that I can be moved to approach

Is Mass still an obligation?

To put the question thus is to think that Mass started off as an obligation. No. It was begun as an act of love: love of Christ and love of our brothers and sisters gathered together in Christ's name.

When this double love had grown cold, recourse had to be had to obligations, and this obligation began at a definite date: 1215, at the Council of the Lateran. (Medieval Christianity did not possess all the virtues!)

An obligation is useful when one's appetite is lacking. "You must eat this," says holy mother the Church to us. But she hopes that we will soon regain our appetite! That is what is happening right now. People are re-discovering the hunger for the Mass. Fewer people attend; but they are volunteers.

Instead of insisting on the obligation, especially in the training of young people, it is better to concentrate on love, and hence give them such an idea of Mass that they may want to attend it. We love! In the history of Christian's love for the Mass, the times of obligation and sanction (mortal sin) indicated a great empty space. We came from love, and we go back to love.

any member of the assembly who is, like myself, a member of the "total Christ." Then the liturgy is not merely a fine chorus of human voices, a human harmony of gestures, but the one voice and aspiration of the Body into which the Holy Spirit has inserted each one of us. My neighbor at church is not just my neighbor, but my "body." Both of us, all the fifty, or the thousand of us, gathered at that moment and in that place, are a Body which is one because it is fed by the Spirit, by the word, and the Bread. Christ would say, "take my body so as to become my body." Nothing in the world — not work, sports, politics, music, not even love — can unite us as Christ unites us by making us one Body with him, a Body of which he is the head. But this is an experience which can be offered only to faith, and lived only in faith.

This shows us how much liturgical prayer is the prayer of Christ. We are never borne more powerfully and more surely towards the Father than when Christ himself makes himself the leader of this prayer of his brothers and sisters. The Holy Spirit can combine closely in our hearts the two essential sentiments which place our prayer in line with Christ's: adoration and charity.

Once one has firmly grasped that authentic liturgical prayer is the prayer of the Body of Christ, the other difficulties of participating appear less important.

There is the proper proportion between words and silence. If those who lead the prayer don't dare to ask the assembly for a few moments of silence, they will rush to fill all the blank spaces with words and music, and the contemplative souls (more numerous than you might think) will have a hard time keeping their prayer alive within. For after all, this is what counts: each one should be able to pray interiorly, not to isolate himself, but to remain united with God in the midst of a little group, within a larger parish community, and even in a huge throng.

Should we speak of boredom? Here is the alibi-reaction of those over twelve: "I don't go because it bores me." This can be true for everybody else as well: singing which is not pleasing, often because the hymns are not well known; homilies that are too long or that are simply verbose; and the Eucharistic Prayer, which is very beautiful, but gives the impression that the celebrant is celebrating all by himself. It is especially when the liturgy of the word has been very lively that the liturgy of the eucharist itself seems boring.

Criticizing a liturgical service may often be useful, on condition that we are willing to do our share. "What can I do to make things better?" Purely negative criticism (always so easy) discourages people with good will and turns aside possible participants.

Especially the young. We cannot drag adolescents to Mass when we ourselves are only mildly motivated; and this is something they feel. An examination into our own liturgical vitality can change many things. For instance, I am always surprised to hear some Christians sigh: "I don't pray." And yet they go to Mass! After a discussion with them I realized that they really don't see that the Mass is a prayer, that it could be the time and place for their best prayer. And from Sunday to Sunday the most effective school of prayer.

Perhaps we should get down to the root of our decision to go to Mass. Is it to fulfill a duty? to assist at a spectacle? and therefore to go "where things keep moving"? Why not? But this is not enough to make of the Mass and of all liturgy "our prayer in Jesus Christ." Where are we more certain to be praying with him, through him and in him?

That is what St. Ignatius of Antioch (died in 110) said in his letter to the Ephesians:

Thus, in the unity of your sentiments and the harmony of your charity you sing to Jesus Christ. Each one, with all the rest becomes a choir, so that in the harmony of your concord, adopting the melody of God in unity, you sing for the Father with one voice through Jesus Christ. Then the Father will listen to you and will recognize in you the members of his Son. Let no one be deceived: if anyone is not within the sanctuary he is depriving himself of God's bread. For since the prayer of two disciples together is so powerful, how much more so that of the whole Church?

When we enter into this view of faith, liturgical prayer considered as the prayer of Christ and of the Church, we feel ourselves urged to participate better.

One very simple means of living our Sunday Mass in greater depth is to draw more help from our missal. It gives us much more than one might think. Not only the texts used in the Mass, but presentations and commentaries, with the possibility of preparing ourselves for Mass, and sometimes of coming back during the week on the Bible texts or on the Eucharistic Prayer. In this way we can get to church like someone alive, like a hundred such people, with whom the celebrant and all those leading the service can achieve what they hope to achieve, a praying assembly.

Praying like Mary, and with Mary

How did Mary pray? No need for much imagination here; we have it all down in black and white in the gospel. She said: *Fiat.* She said: *Magnificat.* She *"pondered all these things in her heart"* and *"she stood at the foot of the cross."* If we place ourselves at her school, what a pathway to prayer will she not show us! Especially if we think that Mary wants to promote a life of prayer in us, and that she can do so.

Fiat. Saying "yes" to God. Every prayer can reach this "yes" even if it has to drag itself there. We find the same lesson in Gethsemane: *"Not my will but yours be done!"* But with a difference. When she said her *fiat* Mary could not measure how far that "yes" would take her. Her prayer is like a blank check.

Her prayer will soar up in the *Magnificat*, in exultation. "How wonderful life is with you, O Almighty One!" Mary teaches us how to pray exultingly. Our blank check given to God is not really serious unless it is signed by a generally happy and trustful person, even if at certain moments saying *Magnificat* means believing in a love which is hard to believe in. Once I heard the *Magnificat* sung at the funeral of a twelve-year-old girl; but what a death was hers, and what faith was theirs!

This cannot be an isolated cry, suddenly bursting forth from time to time, from a desert of not praying. One's whole life must secretly be a *fiat* so that now and then a *Magnificat* may burst forth. This is where we re-discover Mary, the great contemplative, who keeps poring over the enigma of life in her heart. We can understand how in this continual meditation, in that interior occupation, there could be engendered the *fiat* and the *Magnificat,* and the silent strength that kept Mary standing at the foot of the cross.

By inviting us to meditate on life's happenings, Mary teaches us the lesson of patience. We sometimes tend to forget how much she had to wait. Thirty years of obscurity at Nazareth — and he was the Messiah! As a Jewish woman she would have expected something more exciting! We can feel this at Cana. As soon as she senses that things are about to start happening, she nudges her Son a bit. But quickly she drops back into new and demanding patience. She stays clear of the excitement, and comes close to him again only when sorrows begin to lower. Jesus alone can

---

The earliest prayer to Mary

This was found on an Egyptian papyrus, which seems to go back to the second century. It eventually became our "We fly to your patronage..."

Under the protection of your mercy we take refuge, holy Mother of God. Do not disdain our prayers when we suffer difficulties, but save us from all danger, O glorious and blessed Virgin.

---

know to what an extent she keeps herself in the disposition of her *fiat,* of "doing the will of the Father," and it is in that, he tells us, that she is truly his mother. By praying at her side we shall acquire patience and courage to say *fiat* repeatedly. It is a very short prayer, but one which so powerfully transforms us.

Praying at her side? It all happens, it would seem, by osmosis. Saying the rosary means remaining near her and feeling that her sentiments are filling our hearts until we truly become the children of her noble heart.

Praying at her side, and, for instance, before her icon with the changing eyes. Try it yourself. One day we can read in her look a tender peace: "Be quiet, the road is rough, but it leads up to the light." Another day we may perceive a note of anxiety in her gaze: "Might you not be the one with whom God might do great things?"

The last word that we read in the New Testament about Mary shows her to us in prayer. *"Together they devoted themselves to constant prayer. There were some women in their company, and Mary, the mother of Jesus"* (Acts 1:14). "With some women and Mary . . ." Here again it is a case of osmosis. She does not preside; she does not teach, but near her all are of one heart, together, assiduous, and they are getting ready for the event of Pentecost. It seems to me that prayer with Mary is this side-by-side presence. "Now, at this present moment," so that we may remain very close to her "at the hour of our death."

Praying like Mary; praying with Mary . . . Can I not dare to say, "praying to Mary?" Of course we can say it, and I do say it; but pointing out right away the immense difference between praying to Mary and praying to God.

Praying to God means praying to the Father through Christ and in the Holy Spirit. Praying to Mary means directing our prayers to God through her hands, as for instance the Church says at the offertory on August 15: *Lord, while the Most Blessed Virgin Mary who was taken up to heaven intercedes for us, may our hearts long to rise up to you.*

There you have all the purity and power of Marian devotion. It is not an intimate conversation with Mary. She herself is only for God and leads us to him. She is never, therefore, the final word of our prayers. God alone is the summit. But she can be, in our scaling of the mountain, the anchor-person on the mountaineers' rope by her example and her help. Hers is the most effective prayer of intercession; this is nearly always the word used in the liturgy to speak of her power in our regard.

Grant, O Lord, through the glorious intercession of Mary that we may share in the fullness of your grace (3d Mass of the Common of the Most Blessed Virgin).

We see very clearly Mary's place. She is not the fullness, but she is near it. She is not the source of grace, but a loving and admirable mother who can and will draw from the source. To pray to Mary is to implore the help of her hands which are so full because of God's infinite love for her. No other creature is so close to him, and so close to us. Repositioned within our movement towards God, our prayer to Mary can take many forms: fixed, like the rosary, or very spontaneous. We can never find anything better than the oldest prayer, which dates back to the third century. Mary who spoke so little must love this reticent prayer:

We fly to your patronage, O holy mother of God. Do not let us who pray to you succumb to temptation, but deliver us from danger, O you, alone pure and blessed one.

The Angelus

Illustrated by Millet's celebrated painting, the Angelus was fully adopted in 1588 (in the Manuale Catholicorum of St. Peter Canisius). Abandoned for a while it is making a comeback these days with its simplicity, purity and richness. This short prayer said morning, noon and night, brings our thoughts back to God at these important moments of each day. Very much gospel-inspired and marial, it reminds us of the Christian mystery par excellence, the Incarnation; and it teaches us to pray to Mary in highly accurate theological terms.

The Angel of the Lord announced to Mary
that she would be the mother of the Savior;
and she conceived by the Holy Spirit.
Hail Mary. . .

Behold the handmaid of the Lord;
let it be done to me according to your word.
Hail Mary. . .

And the Word was made flesh,
and dwelt among us.
Hail Mary. . .

Pray for us, O holy mother of God, that we may be made worthy of the promises of Christ.

Let us pray: Pour forth, we beseech you, O Lord, your grace into our hearts, so that we to whom the Incarnation of your Son our Lord Jesus Christ was made known by the message of an angel, may by his Passion and Cross be brought to the glory of his Resurrection, through Jesus Christ, our Lord. Amen.

III.
UNION WITH GOD,
THE SEED-BED OF PRAYER

I get lost in everything that is being said about prayer, and in all that is being put forward these days as prayers; so I began to think that there must be some kind of common bed-rock, a common source, a key to it all. I hunted for the idea, the word, the truth from which the very essence of prayer would emerge — something that must be included in every prayerful act.

I think I have found it: union with God. Union with God is the seed-bed in which all prayer must germinate and spring up. That may seem perfectly obvious, my poor fellow! Of course prayer means uniting oneself with God. But is this so very sure? Why then do distraction and routine (both the opposite of union) so generally make their appearance in the landscape of prayer? Why can we recite so many Our Fathers and even celebrate Mass without really having encountered God? Why do we so often settle for aping a union that does not exist?

The great inversion

The answer to all this seems evident, too; we don't seek such union with God enough; *our efforts are too insufficient.*

It was at this point that something I read turned my thinking inside out: *Behold the Spirit* by Alan Watts. In this book, although it contains a good many questionable points, I found the key to prayer, or rather the seed-bed from which it springs. "We don't need to look for God; he is here already, right now. We do not need to *achieve* the state of union with God; it is already given to us."

That really changed my thinking. Prayer thus becomes, essentially, gaining awareness of our union with God, and secondarily inventing forms of prayer which exercise that union and reinforce it. We don't pray in order to unite ourselves with God; we pray because we are already united with God. Union is something given, but it has to be lived.

We thus come back to Jesus in what constitutes him and in what he wishes to give us as the basic ingredient in our prayer: *"my Father and I are one."* Prayer is gaining consciousness of this union in unity, and one means of living it intensely. The other means, which must be stressed over and over, is the conforming of our will with his: *"I always do what pleases him"* (Jn 8:29).

Making efforts to pray now seems to me an initial mistake. We think too much *first of all* about our courage which wishes to make something happen, or to conquer something, whereas *first of all* that something is already given to us; it is only afterwards that we must live by our courage. The specialists call this the "counter gift" or "response."

Thus, the gift and the courage to use it must always join to make up our relationship with God. If we are not conscious of the gift, our courage goes astray; this can be seen in the many failures in prayer; but without courage God's gift would remain an unexploited treasure.

Thus, prayer is a struggle; but we must make no mistake here; the battle has to be fought in union with God. Otherwise, we would end up with this all-too-frequent paradox: praying . . . while remaining far from God! We do all sorts of things, while neglecting to plant the seed of our prayer, whatever kind of prayer it may be, in the seed-bed of union with God, which alone can engender true prayer: "you are here, Lord, and I am here too; we are one."

Prayer makes use of union with God. Once we have

reached this basic conviction, there is still a journey to undertake involving both theory and practice.

— we need to understand the gift of union, and believe in it;

— we need to become conscious of this union;

— we need to find practical measures enabling us to live by this union.

God in us

I am going to speak of things we all know, very certain truths, very well-founded principles; and yet they seem to us so impressive, so strange even, that we stay apart from them, somewhat embarrassed. "God dwells in us." There you have it; these few words say everything. But what do we do about such a truth?

Perhaps we should, first of all, go over the basics found in the extraordinary secrets Jesus told us.

"I am in the Father, and you in me, and I in you. . . . If anyone loves me, he will keep my word, and my Father will love him and we will come and make our abode with him" (Jn 14:20-21). *"Abide in me, and I in you"* (Jn 15:4).

To give a more technical expression to this gift of God's presence within us, we use the word "inhabitation." Others use the expression "state of grace," which has the disadvantage of suggesting something static whereas we are dealing with a dynamic presence within us. God within us can only be a love that acts, or that seeks to act, in the measure of our cooperation.

Yes, this is how God loves us. This is not imagination, dreamland, but revelation. We must absolutely come to believe this to the point of living by it. We must leave aside the notion of conquering our union with God, and grasp the idea of exploiting all the riches of this treasure. Union with God is given to us now. God is not waiting for us in heaven, or at the culmination of gigantic efforts. He is already here.

Elizabeth of the Trinity is an example for us on this

point, and speaks persuasively. "I leave you my faith in the presence of God, that God who is all love and who dwells in our souls. This intimacy with him within was the shining sun that lit up my life" (Letter #333). "Think that you are in him, that he makes himself your abode here below; and then that he is in you, that you possess him in the depths of your being; that at any hour of the day or night, in all your joys and trials, you can find him there, close at hand, within. This is the secret of happiness" (Letter #175).

This is also the secret of prayer, the seed-bed of prayer. This union is always possible, because it is always given to us. Nothing causes this union, since it is a gift; but everything should flow from it, starting with our life of prayer. Now that's really something new! Praying means regaining consciousness of our union with God, and living a moment of love with *love* within us. You may call this mental prayer or petition, psalms or rosary, alleluia and even cries and reproaches. You may call it praying in secret, or celebrating mass liturgies. But it is always finding union once again.

Prayer is a tryst of love

With regard to prayer, where do you stand?

—on the level of prayer-duty? Sunday Mass . . . evening prayer? Is it truly a loving encounter with God? Perhaps you're on the level of forgotten prayer. You have nothing against prayer, but time has gone by, you don't pray anymore; you have forgotten God.

—if you are on the level of "prayer as a dream" (I would like to pray, but what do I need to do?) think that the beginning of prayer is a cry of love.

—prayer is above all loving. Then prayer goes on to nourish love. We must pray as we love, and make every prayer a tryst of love.

P. Jacquemont

Becoming aware of union with God

So what do current expressions mean, like "asking for love" or "begging for grace," or even appeals like: "Come!" or "Draw me to you!" since he is already there in us? We can't tell God, "give me your love"; what else has he to give? If we exist at all, it is because God has loved us; his presence is one of love; our union is in love.

But here we encounter the second great notion of a spirituality of union. The first step was: "union is given to us"; the second is: "we must make an effort to become aware of this union and to live accordingly."

"I was thinking, O Lord," wrote St. Augustine, "of your gifts; seeds which in the hearts of your faithful produce such amazing harvests" (*Confessions* 9:11).

What have we harvested from our union with God? What do we do about God's dwelling in us? Whither do we wander when we go off to pray far from his presence, that is, without thinking of him, without renewing our awareness of his presence?

This second step, becoming aware, is obviously of major importance. We need to go on from the simple, scarcely conscious realization of God's presence, to a life lived together with him, a life as wide awake as possible. Here we encounter a word made popular by oriental spirituality: "awakening." In fact, every prayer should be the awakening of an attention which will make our union with God truly active.

Thus we shall progress into the reality of this union; we shall not remain bogged down in discourses and methods which encourage us intellectually and emotionally, but which do not really make us live this union with God. What Jesus tells us in John 15:4, *"Abide in me, and I in you,"* is not a word uttered carelessly; it is a precious and concrete exhortation. Since this indwelling is given to you, become aware of it; live it; do not seek to pray outside of such a gift of union.

But what, precisely, is this awareness, which matters so

much for our prayer? Above all, we must not be hypnotized by the idea of some kind of "feeling." Not that all feeling must be banished from our relationships with God. Sometimes (fortunately!) he gives us the feeling of his presence and action; but this is something we must accept without having sought it.

Nor should we think of an effort in the sense of a direct and full intellectual knowledge. Our simple consciousness of existing, our awareness of the moment we are just now living, are not easy to grasp; it is all indirect, fragmentary and imprecise; the present is never given to us independently of what it produces or contains.

In fact, (and here I am once more following the lead of Alan Watts, and using his words) in this domain we must go beyond our usual fashion of thinking and feeling; we are on a level of reality which we experience without being able to explain it clearly, still less to imagine it. One might think that there is really nothing here, and that this much touted union with God is something we really cannot utilize; but here we need to rely on the experience of the saints. Their awareness of their union with God is such that it explains the amount of time and the intensity they devoted to their prayer, even when they were busiest about many other things. To hunger for prayer is a call arising from our union with God, and it already makes us aware of that union.

While we cannot come to grips with it directly, our becoming aware of our union with God demonstrates its reality in the three effects it produces. First of all an unmistakable climate of peace: "You are here, and I am here." This certainty brings along with it liberty, security and joy.

Another effect: love is lived precisely in that which affords the happiness of love, the intensity of presences. "You are here and I am here."

Finally, we experience the fullness of the present moment, something we need to insist on a bit. Becoming aware of our union with God at first calls for a difficult effort;

then it becomes a simple reflex action deep within ourselves. It brings us face to face with the essence of our life: the present moment, that drop of life. Usually we let the present moment be swept along in a flood of facts, and of things to be done, without paying too much attention to any of them; and so we live a washed-out type of life. We are not, probably, capable of living with constant and ardent attention to all we do. But it would be a pity, really, to let our prayer just wander along, without making it a moment of real intensity in our life. If union with God is always given to us, real communion, alive and fully awake, depends on our awareness in the given instant.

That this instant can be our moment of communion with God is a simple statement, apparently quite banal . . . and yet it is something unheard of, because we so rarely transform that possibility into something real. Thus viewed, all prayer becomes our effort to move from simple union to true communion.

Whence there results a combat which should be implacable, against inattentive prayer. The two words clash when one has understood to what a degree true prayer is the most powerful reflexive grasping of the present moment.

The struggle to live this union with God

We can now affirm that to be a truly lived union, prayer must first of all be attention, a real school of attention. I found in *Les Trois Piliers Du Zen (The Three Pillars of Zen)* by Ph. Kapleau the following anecdote which is worth many disquisitions on the importance of attention in prayer which is truly union.

> *One day, a man of the people said to Ikkyu, the Master of Zen: "Would you be kind enough to write down for me some maxim of the highest wisdom?" Right away Ikkyu took up his brush and wrote, "Attention!" "Is that all?" asked the man. "Would you not add something more?"*

Ikkyu then wrote: "Attention; attention."
Irritated, the man told him: "I really do not find much depth or subtlety in what you have written."
Then Ikkyu wrote the same word thrice: "Attention, attention, attention."
Nearly enraged, the man asked him: "What does that word mean, after all?"
And Ikkyu politely replied: "Attention" means "attention."

To pray, after all, means to become attentive to God, all of a sudden. Now we know, finally, what that means: attention to the union; grasping the union that has been transformed into communion by conscious awareness. Attention to the words, to the gestures, to our neighbors, is evidently good and necessary; but it always runs the risk of making us stop too soon at something that is not God. The effort needed in prayer is that of soaring straight up to the goal, of settling oneself *first of all* if I dare say so, in full union with God. Then, once we are attentive to God we can and should pay attention to what this or that prayer requires of us. But it will be a true prayer! This primary attention to God is our only safeguard against the two falsifications of prayer: routine and mimicry.

Attention is much more than a quality our prayer must have. It *is* prayer because it is communion. But when one wants to pray it is not enough to say to oneself: "Now, I am going to be very attentive!" What is needed is training in what could be called contemplative faith.

Mental prayer is evidently the best school of attention to God. It is essentially the prayer in which we make ourselves present to the Present One; it aims directly at union by refusing the use of our own words or thoughts, in order to receive everything from God himself. "You are here, and I am here in our tryst of love, and I expect all from you." Anyone who has seriously undertaken mental prayer knows quite well that it requires the maximum of attention, and that within us it also prepares us to be attentive to union with God in our other prayers and to the presence of others. Thus, it makes us more truly caring. What do love, counsel and help amount to without being genuinely present to another?

The spirituality of union with God urges us to profit by other "presences" of God which we do not exploit sufficiently. For instance, our meeting with Jesus in the gospel can be practiced as a powerful union with Jesus who wishes to live this or that detail of our daily life. Thus understood, the gospel becomes an apprenticeship for union, and even the true exercise of union with God.

Another place where awareness can be sharpened is in the eucharistic encounters: Mass and adoration of the Most Blessed Sacrament. Here again, what a difference between a Mass heard distractedly, a routine communion, adoration largely made up of daydreams, and a vivid awareness of Christ's presence, and his very clear call: "Give yourself, as I gave myself."

Of course, our effort to be united with God must make us more open to his presence in our neighbors; this is in fact the supreme test of our union. You are truly my son if you are truly their neighbor. Frequent meditation on

---

Islamic prayer
(the beginning of all prayer)

Praise be to God the sovereign of the universe, the clement the merciful one, sovereign of the day of retribution. It is you whom we adore; it is you whose help we implore. Direct us in the right path, in the path of those whom you have filled with your blessings, of those who have not yet provoked your anger, and who do not go astray. Amen.

Sourate 4

Matthew 25:40 will preserve us from an egoistical piety, all bent inward on an unreal "you and I" sort of relationship. Union with the true God gives us God's eyes when we look at our neighbors. Whoever lives a life of love lives it in all circumstances. Attention to the presence of God does not hide him from us in our neighbors. But it is experience which demonstrates all this, not theoretical considerations. The difficulty about talking of union with God arises from the fact that one always seems to be theorizing, whereas one is trying to describe one's own experiences.

The ultimate "contemplative" glance, the most difficult one to bring into our union with God, but perhaps the most necessary of all is attention to God even in the midst of our work.

It is here that most of us are tempted to part company with God. "See you later, God!" This means breaking our life of union up into small bits, and making it extremely difficult for us to put that life back together again. Whoever does not want to remain united with God in everything will find it very difficult to re-create something like "islands of contemplation" where he can find full union again. This is the source of certain failures in mental prayer. We think that we can grab hold of God again on emerging from a huge distraction that hid him from us; but only habitual contact with him makes it possible to find him again and to establish a more intense awareness of him in mental prayer, and even in any prayer.

This reminds me of "zapping" — the new word coined to indicate the use of a remote control device when watching TV. It allows us to tune in one program, to switch to another, to turn the set off, then to turn it back on again. But we have no such "remote control" device to put God at our disposal. We shall find it hard to contact him in our many prayers unless we live with him habitually, in grace and union.

Prayer is not a stranger whom we go to meet while leaving life behind, nor an intruder into our life. Every ordinary life is indeed its habitat. Prayer is nourished by a

Latin American prayer

I came here to pray,
to the temple
filled with people and with lights.

Some lifted up their eyes.
How many will know
the reasons for Christ's wounds?

If you are a Christian,
why do you not see in Christ
the good Brother who for your sake struggled
to teach you how to live unselfishly?

If you belong to Christ,
fulfill your mission.
Gold does not make one rich.

No ownership is recognized in heaven.
Only the soul goes there,
filled with regrets because it failed to live in brotherhood.

Ask Christ
why he keeps his head bowed down,
why his eyes
always gaze on us with sorrow.

Meditate a little,
and you will find the answer.
It is because you do not live in love.

We shall not cease to see him thus,
sad and full of bitterness,
unless we build a brotherly world.

*The prayer of Marina from Colombia, a woman of the people,
mother of seven children, who lives in the* barrio *of Medellin*

sort of variety in the different presences of God; the gospel encounter influences eucharistic vitality, life with others, courageous living, and vice versa. If we never wander far from God, our prayer will easily find union again.

In this way we can escape the scourge which debilitates Christian existence so much: living on the balcony, and living a double life. Living on the balcony means living a superficial, disorganized distracted life because we do not pay attention to God's presences. By requiring depth and attention these presences would develop the contemplative life in us. Prayer from the balcony is only an imitation. While all true prayer should spring from within, here one simply simulates from the outside both attention and fervor.

Many difficulties in prayer come from this inversion of prayer's true movement. We want to go from the balcony to prayer; whereas we should first ensconce ourselves in union with God (which is always accessible from the outset, and always offered to us); and then, starting from this interior reality let our prayers flame out. Let us not hook prayers onto our lives from the outside; let us make them spring forth from the deep sharing of our life with that of God. Fr. Caffarel teaches this in a strikingly suggestive manner. One must not, he says, be a Christmas tree, because a Christmas tree is a dead tree on which people hang a lot of things which will forever remain foreign to it. We should be living trees which produce life, flowers and fruit. Prayer which springs from our inmost being is the fruit of a healthy, living tree.

I mentioned another danger which threatens us: leading a double life. When we confine our contemplative life to the few moments of explicit prayer we make of it a sort of "sacred island" lost in the vast ocean of our active life. This points us straight to a double failure. Prayer separated from life becomes boring and withers away. Activity without union with God transforms us into pagans. Nothing but the perpetual renewal of union unifies our life, which then becomes entirely God's own.

All that we have been saying about union with God will remain unreal and of no consequence if we lack what Jesus always joins very closely to prayer: a certain type of faith without which our prayer becomes agitated or soporific, while remaining far from true union.

All of us have an ordinary faith; but to pray well, that is not enough. Oh, of course we say a lot of prayers. But what has become of our union with God? It is found only where faith rises above the ordinary. "I believe, Lord, that I am always in contact with you by your grace. I believe that you dwell in me, and that praying means becoming aware of that presence, and then living everything else together with you!"

What faith! Not only to say such words, but to make them the source of all else: our relationships with God and with others, and our work. We pray in order to discover that source, and to be able to find it always in spite of the hubbub of life, with its distractions and worries. "I believe that you are here; I trust totally in these revealing words which tell me that I am in you and you are in me. I don't want to pray any more without a vivid awareness of your presence."

IV.
APOSTOLIC PRAYER

During an interview with Cardinal Decourtray I asked him: "Why must we keep repeating to Christians 'you must be apostles' ?"

We have to avoid being deceived about "we must"

"We are mistaken about those 'you must' expressions," he answered. "It is, moreover, a mistake frequently committed in Christianity. We think, first of all, of an effort of will: 'you must do this; you must do that; you must think of others; you must be an apostle.' But nowadays people (the young ones especially) come back at you with the question: 'Why?' "

"How do you answer them?"

"By bringing in Christ, first of all. Apostolic passion can be inspired only by a passionate love of Christ." This reminded me of what brought about the tremendous unity of Christian life in Fr. d'Alzon, the founder of the Assumptionists. On the first page of his *Directory* he wrote: "Christ is my life." And at the end: "I cannot love Jesus Christ without wanting everybody else to love him; and there you have the apostolic characteristic of my life." I must first be passionately devoted to Christ; and then I must make others share in my passion. In this context, "must" is the correct word, because it is in its place, the second place. Given that, the will, the decision, the action will follow from the passion, and we shall find ourselves involved in a flaming "must." In this I am following

Christ, who was passionately concerned about his Father and his kingdom. *"I have come to light a fire on the earth. How I wish the blaze were ignited!"* (Lk 12:49). Previously, he had said: *"I must announce the good news of the reign of God"* (Lk 4:42). These words obviously sprang from his enthusiasm for the Good News. How well he knew why it was truly the Good News, and why he had to go everywhere proclaiming it.

The same passion made Paul say: *"Preaching the gospel is not the subject of a boast. . . . I am ruined if I do not preach it"* (1 Cor 9:16). The other apostles too had declared: *"It is impossible for us to refrain from speaking"* (Acts 4:20). All this is far removed from a "must" imposed from without; it is rather the eruption of an inner volcano.

Thus we are referred back to the source of apostolic inspiration. The constant danger, as Cardinal Decourtray said, is to forget this source while worrying a lot about the channels. But what is the use of the innumerable "you must" injunctions of the evangelizing strategists and the pastoral structures, if all the channels remain empty of the living waters of a genuine passion for Christ?

Apostolic prayer is first of all contemplation. What can we say about Christ if we are not burning with love for him? and if we do not perceive how much the world suffers from the cold? Indeed, this is why apostolic prayer is first of all a double contemplation: of Christ, and of the world; this is its first step.

Like all passions, our passion for Christ is aroused and grows through knowledge, in loving encounters which vary depending on situations, tastes, and age. For instance, while simply reciting the rosary we can do nothing more pleasing to Mary than to ask her unceasingly to help us know her Són better.

In the same way, reading the gospel can be an ardent contemplation. *"Were not our hearts burning inside us as he talked to us on the road?"* (Lk 24:32). And of course, exegesis and Christology can also become, if one so desires, moments of contemplation.

In mental prayer, especially, Jesus reveals himself, when we are totally attentive. "I hope for all from you."

But I think we should insist particularly on our eucharistic encounters: Mass and adoration. The silence of the Host speaks to us. This sign of a "life given over" makes us willing to accept all the crosses that accompany every apostolate. It prepares us for the difficult career of a "buried life," because it strengthens our faith in the silent but active presence of Christ.

This was Fr. de Foucauld's missionary school. "Let us sanctify all the mission lands through this presence of Jesus in the Host, and of his adorers." We should not think here of a static, passive presence, but of a Christic activity, a focussing of divine energy. Alas! This resource is so little used because there is so little contemplative faith. Fr. de Foucauld always speaks of Christ's *life* in the holy eucharist. His *life*!

If all humanity cannot be Christian, it can be Christic. No apostle should ignore or forget (yet it happens so often) this doctrine so clearly affirmed in the well-known passages of *Gaudium et Spes* and *Lumen Gentium*. When I cite these to very diversified audiences they are glad to hear the immense horizons of God's activity going on today.

> *The Christian receives the Spirit who makes him capable of accomplishing the new law of love. This is true not only for those who believe in Christ, but also for all men of good will, in whose hearts, invisibly, grace is at work. Indeed, since Christ died for all, and since the ultimate vocation of men is really one, i.e. divine, we must believe that the Holy Spirit offers to all, in ways that only God knows, the possibility of being associated with the paschal mystery.*

And in *Lumen Gentium* we read:

> *Those who have not yet received the gospel are also associated to the Kingdom of God in various ways . . . . Even those who still seek in darkness and under images a God whom they do not know, are not far from God since he gives to all life, breath and all*

71

things, and wills that all men be saved. Those who through no fault of their own are ignorant of the gospel of Christ and of his Church, but who yet seek God with a sincere heart and try, under the influence of his grace, to act in such a way as to fulfill his will as their conscience reveals it to them, can certainly reach eternal salvation.

Even to those who, through no fault of their own, have not yet reached an express knowledge of God, but who labor, not without the help of divine grace, to live an upright life, divine Providence does not refuse the necessary helps for salvation. Indeed, whatever can be found that is good and true among them, the Church considers as a preparation for the gospel and as a gift of the one who enlightens every man, so that finally he may find life.

What an invitation to contemplate the world with truly apostolic eyes! We can breathe deeply when we see that our Church does not allow us to say that any person is excluded from the influence of grace. She makes us attentive to all the many active presences of Christ, to those invisible redemptive activities which should haunt our prayer.

As an apostle I am "someone who is sent out." But to whom? Here again we are dealing with a passion constantly fed by contemplation. We need to look at the world with the eyes of God, while we read John 3:16 in the present tense: *"God so loves the world that he gives it his own Son."* The apostle who accepts that fully, and mulls over it in his prayer, comes to see these men and women whom God so loves in a different light. Even if he cannot always speak to them about his love, at least he tries to be the sign thereof, through all his ways of acting, and through his unshakable confidence. If you only knew what kind of Father you have in heaven (cf. Mt 6:25-34).

The paschal mystery is the great light for every apostolic contemplation. A world is dying. Let us set aside all ineffective nostalgia. A world is being born; let us reject the suspicions which would make us a burden, and the simplistic views which would trivialize us. We go forward among the dying and the newborn, to be for both the word of Christ, the hands of Christ, the courage of Christ in spite of opposition and suffering. The first task of our apostolic prayer is to transform our hearts, come what may, into the heart of Christ.

Prayer in the midst of action safeguards our action

The second mission of apostolic prayer is to permit us to maintain a contemplative attitude even in the midst of action. Action blinds us; we lose the overall picture; we charge into our tasks; we get discouraged; we take refuge in criticism. For such lives, all ups and downs, the pause for prayer is not a luxury. Without it we shall be entrapped by the very means we make use of, and even by our own generosity. The great game of balancing the interior with the exterior is not easy. This brings us to the eternal problem, one which Fr. Varillion observed so well: how to combine depth with breadth in our activity. "We run the risk of losing in extension what we gain in depth (hence, watch out for prayer which becomes a refuge). But we are also constantly threatened with losing in interior strength what we gain on the surface." It is especially, as we have seen, through prayer that the apostle can keep his life very open without losing the interior spirit. Nothing is more helpful, in this regard, than a long period spent with Christ.

Coming back to Christ is as necessary during action as it is before action, because of the basic rule for apostolic effort: "If you want to talk about Christ, be another Christ." People today can be cruel when they see the gulf between what we say and what we do. We can proclaim effectively only what we actually live. In the midst of our action a brief but very fervent examination of conscience will safeguard our action. "Do I really believe what I am about to do or say? What am I really trying to live?" Inevitably Paul's words will keep ringing in our ears. Can we say like him, *"To me, life is Christ"* or, *"It is Christ who lives in me."* This will bring us time after time to a more modest attitude and to greater effort, but those whom we wish to persuade will surely feel, in this case, that we are honestly trying to live up to what we preach.

"We aren't asking you to be a saint," said some young fellows to their chaplain; "all we ask is that you try to be one."

Perhaps this is our first prayer: "O Lord, give me the grace to try to be what I ask others to be."

An apostle cannot be narcissistic

The third role of apostolic prayer is the one most familiar to us: intercession. I shall take as models two great intercessors: Abraham and Moses.

Interceding for Sodom, Abraham said: *"I am presuming to speak to my Lord"* (Gn 18:27). Presuming? No. He prays thus because he lives very close to the Lord, and because he wants to save the Sodomites at any cost.

The apostle's intercessory prayer will never be overbold unless he is very familiar with God and very close to his brothers and sisters. Since this is the prayer of a mediator, he must at the same time dare all with God and feel most keenly the sorrows of people . . . to the point of saying foolish things to God because the sufferings of people crush his heart. *"I could even wish to be separated from Christ for the sake of my brothers"* (Rom 9:3).

What an apostolic grace it would be if on the one hand we shared God's compassion, and on the other experienced a passionate interest in every person we encounter. Can one even imagine a narcissistic apostle? We must constantly check to see if our prayer is indeed filled with concern for others, penetrated by everything that is going on around us and in the world. To see if in spite of the worst news it remains the cry of *a faith that does not falter* as Jesus said. A faith capable of making God arise: *"Because they rob the afflicted, and the needy sigh, now will I arise. I will grant safety to him who longs for it"* (Ps 12:6).

74

An Indian prayer for peace

The calumet was given to my people for peace and friendship. Today we have gathered here to pray for world peace. So I offer it to you, my brothers and sisters.

By using this pipe to signify the presence of the creator and all his creation, we offer this pipe to the Great Spirit, to our mother the earth, and to the four winds.

I am going to pray that we may undertake to pray and to work for peace in our families, in our tribes and our nations. I pray for all our brothers and sisters who walk upon the face of the earth, our mother.

O Great Spirit, with this calumet, the symbol of peace, reconciliation and brotherhood, we beg you to be among us and to bless us today.

O Great Spirit of my fathers, help me to spread your deep desire and your message. Help me to be just and kindly.

If my brothers and sisters are weak and hesitant, give me good thoughts and show me how I can help them.

O Great Spirit, I beg for your blessings. I ask that you give peace to all my brothers and sisters in this world. I ask you to make us understand how to live like brothers and sisters, and to love one another.

O Great Spirit, I lift my pipe to you, to your messengers, the four winds. Give us wisdom to teach our children how to love, so that they may grow up with peace in their minds. Teach us to share all the good things you provide us with on this earth.

O Great Spirit, bless all of us here today.

John Pretty, an Indian from Montana, at the Assisi gathering, October 27, 1986.

The apostle is that intercessor who obtains salvation. What salvation? Rarely will he know; and that is why he needs faith of an uncommon kind, which will make his prayer a powerful one, and in its turn his prayer will reinforce his faith. We clearly see this "circular motion" in the saints who were the most insistent pleaders. They harass God by their faith; and this harassment itself builds up their faith, not only when they visibly get what they ask for, but because they thereby gain an assurance which, as we have seen, would be laughable without faith. *"Believe that you will receive whatever you ask for in prayer, it shall be done to you"* (Mk 11:24).

One is not an intercessor just by saying so. Too many of those "I'll pray for you's" are uttered without thinking, and thus downgrade the very idea of prayer. When these words come from a heart very sure of God, and hence very sure of prayer, the promise to pray for someone binds the intercessor very deeply.

Moses' apostolic prayer had another angle to it. He too understood very well God's love and compassion. *"I have witnessed the affliction of my people"* (Ex 3:7). This passionate love for the whole people established between Moses and God an extraordinary connivance.

When God, disgusted with that people, offers to make Moses the leader of another, the latter exclaims: *"But Lord, this is your people!"*

Listening to a man who dares to teach God patience and love is probably one of the high points of an apostolic meditation on the Bible. "Yes, this people has faults; but it is still your people. As for me, I don't want any other one."

What apostle has not been tempted to wish he had a different people to lead; or to grow disenchanted with it as a people, and to concentrate on this or these individuals? Moses, for his part, has come to see things in this grandiose perspective: human beings are loved by God as a people. He never ceases running from the one to the others, speaking about God to the people, and speaking to God about the people. Let us hear him say "your people," and "your God." These two heart-cries will always mark the true apostle.

Actually, he will have a hard time making the people admit that they really are God's people. This for two reasons: they are much too individualistic; and for them, God is the "great absent one." The absence of God? Can we imagine such an idea in Moses, who saw God ever present, day and night, guiding and forming his people? In these chapters of the Bible our intercession will come to rediscover its double dimension: God present in a people to be gathered together. As the third Eucharistic Prayer says: *"You constantly gather your people together."*

The extension of this word "people" takes on fantastic proportions when we think of all humanity marching on, from its beginning to the end of time. Christians, alas, for a long time seemed to be a separate group, until there resounded the extraordinary prologue of *Gaudium et Spes* which proclaimed the close solidarity of the Church with the whole human family:

> *The joys and the hopes, the sorrows and the anguish of people today, especially of the poor and suffering, are also the joys and hopes, the sorrows and the anguish of the disciples of Christ; and there is nothing truly human which does not find an echo in their hearts. Their community, indeed, is made up of men, gathered in Christ, conducted by the Holy Spirit, marching towards the Father's kingdom, bearing a message of salvation which they must proclaim to all. The Christian community, then, recognizes that it is really and intimately united in solidarity with the whole human race and its history.*

At this point a danger threatens the apostle. He may be tempted to say to God, "The human race is your people, but not mine; I can only love a small community."

This is a reaction which can vary from one temperament to another. The protagonists of "close to home" charity soon begin to look upon the visionaries of "far off charity" as dreamers. But can an apostle stay on the sidelines of God's all-embracing designs?

If God at first chose a small people, and then a much larger one, it was in the last analysis in favor of all humanity, who some day will be his people, and so are his people today.

But is this "openness to all humanity" possible to put into practice all the time? Certainly, it is difficult for an apostle and for even a very apostolic community to avoid concentrating on some restricted sphere of action. Meanwhile, our intercession constantly widens the space of the tent until it includes the whole human family. As we emerge from this all-embracing prayer let us at least pay attention to one requirement which should no longer appear entirely mythical to us: "You are a human being, so you belong to my people."

Apostolic prayer keeps us working at God's task

It was a priest of the Paris Foreign Missions who led me to discover one aspect of apostolic prayer about which we think too little.

In the *Bulletin of the Miraculous Medal* he was meditating on his prayer as a super-active missionary: here a chapel; there a dispensary; yonder an orphanage. . . .

We pray for what we call *our* apostolate, meaning by that our various good works. This is absolutely necessary; we need God's light and help; our prayer is a proof of our faith. *"Without me you can do nothing"* (Jn 15:5). So we pray that our good works may be blessed; but not to make God bless *our* pet schemes! I propose a project; I plan a course of action, and I say: "Lord, please bless all this." I hire God as a worker on my building site, whereas I am supposed to be working on *his* building site. Prayer must help me to remain united to the Lord vitally enough to attend to his business, not just to mine.

Here again, take Moses, totally involved in God's concerns, never in his own. When we remember the narcissistic delight inseparable from all action (and apostolic work cannot avoid this), how could we fail to think that only very special prayer can make us avoid putting ourselves, without realizing it, on our own payroll?

Praying on the hilltop

Sometimes very active people end up by not believing much in prayer. As they rarely read the Bible, they no longer catch its message (so clear, however): "Nothing without God's strength." For instance, take the example of Gideon among many others.

He had been assured of God's help in his battle against the Madianites. Still, Gideon had called together the whole people. But the Lord told him: *"There are too many of you; Israel might glory at my expense and say, 'it was my own hand that saved me!' "* (Jgs 7:2-22). Finally, Gideon overcame with only three hundred men . . . plus God.

So that he may never think: "It is my own hand that saved me; I did it all by myself," the apostle should also re-read the famous story of Moses' arms.

While Joshua was leading the battle against Amalek, Moses climbed to the top of a hill with Aaron and Hur. *"When Moses lifted his hands, Israel overcame; but when he let them drop, Amalek overcame."* Moses' arms grew tired; so Aaron and Hur held them up, and *"Joshua overcame Amalek."*

Moses' outstretched arms are the apostle's prayer. Especially when his mission seems most desperate he is called upon to practice the purest, nakedest faith. Let him not fail in this.

Moses' uplifted arms also represent the prayer that the apostle pleads for from such or such a monastery, from some pious old lady who tells him timidly: "All I can do is pray." What an opportunity to make an act of faith with her: "Don't say, I can only pray; say I am going to pray.

And I tell you that I have nothing left but your prayers to get me out of the mess I'm in."

If we believed more in this "last chance" type of prayer it would provoke a more frequent call for the help of prayer, even when everything seems to be going right. In the apostolate, nothing can ever go right without prayer. But if we keep on repeating this too distractedly, we end up by losing our faith in prayer; we don't enlist the help of those "who can only pray." Yet they would be so happy to make miracles from the top of the hill.

V.

THE STRUGGLES OF PRAYER

Now, where are we? After a bird's eye view of different ways of praying today, we sought lessons from the master of our prayer, Jesus Christ. This led us to consider the depths of Christian prayer, its seed-bed: union with God.

On the way we noted that there were difficulties, struggles. Objections against prayer sprang up unceasingly. Of what use is prayer? And anyway, is it not preferable to act, not better to go out and help people, than to sing alleluia?

To these external objections were added interior difficulties: the nerve-racking battle against distractions; the impression that one is losing one's time — an increasingly rare commodity today.

Are these not struggles which have always existed? Yes, no doubt; but they take on very contemporary guises. New suspicions rise up within us unceasingly. By facing them squarely we shall learn how to help others who are struggling; and we shall be building our own life of prayer on a rock foundation. As it is, it is hard enough to pray; to succeed we need to be very solidly anchored.

1. "Our prayers are never heard"

Today, prayer of petition is questioned more and more. It is no use to pray; you never get what you ask for. Anyhow, doesn't God know everything? Shall we presume to bore him with our jeremiads? And what would it all change? He is the one who never changes; and he cannot

Thoughts on prayer

- Don't pray for God to give you what you want; pray that you may give him what he wants (Quaker prayer).
- Love is a spring that thirsts (Marie Noel).
- Praying is not being intelligent; it means being there.
- All prayer comes down to adoration (you are here), and to petition (help me to be what you expect of me).
- Prayer an escape? Why not, if there we really find God? Lucky escape! From time to time we need a mini-solitude with him. He will bring us back to the essential and then get us going again towards our brothers and sisters.
- Unceasing prayer means remaining constantly in connivance with God.
- Prayer may not always change a situation; but it can change how we see the situation.
- Prayer is like inhaling, which renews the tone of your life; all we do after that is like exhaling.
- Prayer is our faith beginning to speak.
- Personal prayer: I believe in you; liturgical prayer: we believe in you. That "we" changes a lot of things.
- When you pray, you open the shutters to let in God's supernatural light. Let the sunshine in, it's much better than your own shadows.
- Prayer is believing that God is looking at me.
- Prayer should open a space of loving silence in our hearts.
- Speak, Lord, or remain silent. Either way you are here, and so am I.
- Don't dream of a life where you could pray. Pray now!
- God gives the gift of prayer to the one who prays (St. John Climacus).
- What is self-abandonment to God? Not "you are the master," but "you love me."
- Mental prayer? You are here and I am here, and I await all from you.

change anything in this world; his place is not in the real world of everyday life. Another old objection has come back strongly: it's cowardly to beg; it's not proper for a man. We should be able to run our lives. Prayer of petition is too self-interested; the lowest form of prayer. . . .

Operation "Trust"

Before we get involved in this quarrel, it is absolutely necessary to see clearly what is meant by petitioning God. Otherwise, we risk starting discussions that never end, without having defined precisely what we are talking about.

Prayer of petition is not, in the first place, a petition at all, but rather a reply. God is the one who told us *"Ask, and you will receive"* (Mt 7:7). Thus, everything depends on the idea we have of God. Who is this God who tells us to ask? In fairy tales and even in real history certain powerful people say: "Ask me for anything you want." But we know quite well that their power of giving is very limited. They are neither good enough nor mighty enough. If, more or less consciously, we think of God as of someone not quite powerful enough to give us what we ask him, and not so very well-disposed to help us, our request is cankered in its very root.

Prayer follows directly on the notion we have of God. Instinctively when we speak of these things we too readily fall back on ourselves, or on our prayer; but then we cannot escape this manifest fact so damaging to our faith: "God did not hear me!" To say: "Perhaps he answered you in another way," or, "He will grant it to you later," or, "Perhaps you did not pray aright," are all escape hatches which fail to face the real question: Yes, or no, is God a God who grants prayers?

The answer is in John 17:3: *"Eternal life is this: to know you."* By saying this, Jesus thinks of what he sought to reveal to us; what he really came down here for. *"Father, that they may know that you do love them."* Knowing God means just that. How well we know it! But do we draw from this truth all its consequences? When I pray I am praying to someone who loves me, who wants to grant my prayer, and who can do so. Otherwise, what kind of God do I worship?

The importance of our faith in God is seen the minute we start talking about prayer. Has anyone ever met someone who loves, who can grant a legitimate desire, and who refuses to grant it? God would not tell us to ask if he did not want to hear us.

Certain objections against prayer based on human science may not be entirely valueless; but they always spring from human beings and their possible delusions, as though God were not God, and did not tell us unceasingly, "Ask." When we are at last quite sure that it is in God's very nature to hear us, we will be able to sweep clean quite calmly the whole area of prayer of petition; and heaven knows how cluttered up it is!

But the least hesitation about the certainty of being heard risks compromising the whole business. *"You will receive all that you pray for, provided you have faith"* (Mt 21:22). That is what Jesus said. It is not a question here of secondary doubts about the strength of our request, or about its object; the question is about the basic assurance without which all requests are threatened with failure. "I am sure to be heard!" When? How? That may be discussed; but only within the formidable certainty: God is truly God, and he is our God. Starting from that we can face with joyful confidence the real difficulties concerning the conditions, the delays, and the very nature of the granting.

The gospel of answered prayers

Our basic confidence can be built up and made strong with twelve passages that have often been cited. They constitute a sort of gospel of answered prayers. "Ask and you shall receive." Only when one has become fully penetrated by these passages are serious discussions possible; and in them one finds permanent nourishment for one's faith in prayer of petition.

1) Mark 11:24 — *If you are ready to believe that you will receive whatever you ask for in prayer, it shall be done for you.*

We need to insist on this passage, because it is the most forthright, and all Christian existence revolves around it.

The affirmation is clear, brief, uncompromising. Also very disconcerting! It doesn't fit in with all our disappointments. "I prayed so hard, but God did not grant my prayer." But once a person has finally acquired the certainty that God does hear prayers, then no matter what the appearances may be, he can no longer put up with a "God did not listen to me," even the most respectable and the most apparently justified. How many times I wanted to say: "But, believe first of all what he says in Mark 11:24; then you can cry, scream, carry on as much as you want to; but believe, first of all."

Otherwise we may end up with one of the most amazing of all Christian attitudes; some people would rather accept the idea of God's refusing them than the idea that he does listen, even though he repeats it so often.

2) Mark 9:22 — *Everything is possible to a man who trusts.*

This is from the episode of the epileptic child's cure, a key passage in dealing with prayer of petition. Jesus was angry over the lack of faith; and we note the heartrending confidence of the father in his powerful yet humble prayer: "I do believe, but help my lack of trust."

One request following another. Perhaps we should add to our every prayer of petition a plea for more faith in its being heard, since everything depends on having that kind of faith.

3) Matthew 7:7 — *Ask, and you will receive.*

This text breathes hope. It is God calling on our trust; and as far as we are concerned it is our most solid defense against all doubts concerning petitionary prayer. "Say what you like; I myself can see the objections that I can't answer; but I hear even louder what my Father in heaven is telling me: 'Ask!' " And the rest of it: *"Would one of you hand his son a stone when he asks for a loaf, or a poisonous snake when he asks for a fish? If you, with all your sins, know how to give good children what is good, how much more will your heavenly Father give good things to anyone who asks him?"* (Mt 7:9-11).

4) Matthew 18:19 — *If two of you join your voices on earth to pray for anything whatever, it shall be granted you by my Father in heaven.*

This "anything whatever" opens up amazing horizons on the granting of our needs and desires. The starting request matters little. If made with confidence it sets in motion a fulfillment which may turn out to be a real adventure, because it will lift us up even to God's desires. *Give us good things.* Yes, good things for us, but judged so by God, and hence often surprising for our purblindedness. Another insight flows from this passage: the effectiveness of group prayer. Here Jesus speaks of the smallest possible community (why could it not be a married couple, or a pair of friends?) but the principle holds true even more surely for a group, e.g. a group in retreat.

5) Matthew 21:21 — *If you trust and do not falter . . . if you say to this mountain, "Be lifted up and thrown into the sea," even that shall happen.*

"*If.*" That little word on which our Christian life depends so much. *If you do this.* Jesus often says. And as for the granting of our prayers, *if* you doubt not. Back we come to the simile of the rock. We should be so sure that doubt can find no foothold. All the rest, in this area, is very secondary. Practice in asking is above all apprenticeship in not doubting.

6) Luke 11:5-8 and 18:1-8.

Two parables about persistence in prayer. The neighbor whom the man annoys in the middle of the night will end up by giving him what he needs; the judge whom the widow harasses will finally do justice to her. God is neither this annoyed friend nor this unjust judge. What Jesus is trying to teach us here is that we should not pray with feeble requests, soon discouraged. Here he shows us the secret of prayer's effectiveness. It does not act on God, as if he were a deaf Baal (cf. 1 Kgs 18:27), but on ourselves, who need to believe in the power of our pleas with God.

7) Luke 11:13 — *How much more will the heavenly Father give the Holy Spirit to those who ask him.*

Here we see, clearly indicated for us, the true action of prayer. If it is confident enough, and persevering enough, it will obtain the supreme gift: the gift of the Spirit. But since this is always given to us, prayer acts, rather, on our openness to this Gift. He who prays welcomes the inspirations of the Spirit, the power of the Spirit. He places himself under the guidance of the Spirit so as to give direction to his life and to accept the burdens it brings him. Possessing the Spirit, he has everything. If we could only come to understand this verse, we should soon see to what an extent our prayers are "hearable."

8) John 14:13 — *Whatever you ask in my name, I will do.*

Here we have another aspect of prayer which was mentioned above when speaking of Jesus, the master of prayer.

9) 1 John 3:22 — *We will receive at his hands whatever we ask. Why? Because we are keeping his commandments and doing what is pleasing in his sight.*

This shows us how our life is the underpinning of our prayer. "Because we keep his commandments" is very optimistic (as is John's whole letter); it reminds us of the "if" previously mentioned. Our requests will be granted *if* our whole life backs them up. We remain firmly convinced that we shall be heard, but our actions must reinforce our requests. Otherwise we should be practicing magic, which seeks to obtain favors from God without changing anything in our hearts and in our lives. The certainty of being heard is a springboard to further progress, not a reward for laziness or misconduct.

10) 1 John 5:14 — *We have this confidence in God: that he hears us whenever we ask for anything according to his will.*

The same affirmation, more or less, as in the previous text. Our prayer must not be without an effort to please God. But "according to his will" risks cooling off our trust; it sounds too much like thinking of the king's "good pleasure," and of the courtier who wants to flatter him. Away with such images! God is no Louis XIV. Jesus told us often enough that God's "good pleasure" is his love for us. When our prayer strives to conform with his will, it is asking for our happiness from the best connoisseur of what is good for us.

11) James 1:6-7 — *Yet he must ask in faith, nothing doubting, for the doubter is like the surf tossed and driven by the wind. A man of this sort . . . must not expect to receive anything from the Lord.*

An unflattering portrait—typical St. James! But it describes us just as we too often are in our petitionary prayers, wavering between trust and skepticism. We should cut out this useless prayer, or else toil and moil ourselves up to a level of real confidence.

12) Ephesians 3:20-21 — *To him whose power now at work in us can do immeasurably more than we ask or imagine— to him be glory.*

Paul's cry of praise is the best conclusion to all this. God's power to grant our prayers far surpasses all our wildest dreams. Our prayers should be worthy of his magnificence, but we never open our mouths wide enough (cf. Ps 81:11).

To which God are our prayers addressed?

Sure of being heard (this is the guarantee of all petitionary prayer) we can now turn to the objections.

First: why bother God, since he knows everything?

Even Jesus says so: *"Your Father knows what you need before you ask him"* (Mt 6:8).

Yes; but what is Jesus really aiming at here? Pagan insistence. As for religious insistence, he requires it as we have seen; and we always need to balance out his teachings with one another, otherwise people would say he contradicts himself. In fact, while he recommends the right kind of insistence he condemns useless wordiness, which treats God as though he were an idol. *"They [the pagans] think they will win a hearing by the sheer multiplication of words"* (Mt 6:7).

Of course God knows all things; but when people love each other does their knowing each other destroy all dialogue? By our petitions we strengthen our relationships with God. By expressing our needs, repeatedly, in the presence of our Father we sometimes get the impression that he sees things in a different light. The Spirit bends us to his will. In any case, our petitions bring us close to him; they are one aspect of the capital element in all prayer: namely union with God. Saying "you know all" with a tinge of discouragement might end up by locking us into a silence which is very dangerous in love. We might try to keep the flock of our troubles and desires out of God's sight. The elder son in the parable lived with his father without asking for anything; the result was not much to brag about.

A second objection: God does not change.

Here we come up against a very difficult apparent contradiction between the god of the philosophers and the God of the Bible. I say an apparent contradiction, for of course, there is only one God, but two very different ways of approaching him.

For the philosophers, God does not change; he is immutable in his designs and impassible. But this is not the

God revealed to us in the Bible, with his love, his anger, his repentance (cf. Gen 6:6), his unbelievable returns full of pardon and love to David (cf. 2 Sm). Anthropomorphism? No doubt, but much more than that. Whether clumsily or magnificently expressed, the revelation is clear: if God is a God of love, he cannot remain immutable and impassible. He acts; or let's quit calling him a loving God.

Our petition soars up to his love, that unimaginable love which Jesus spoke of in John 3:16. *"God so loved the world that he gave his only Son."* If that means an impassible love we shall have to find other words.

Let the philosophers find their own solutions. The praying Christian knows that his petition establishes a bridge between time and the eternal, and causes the immutable one to move. The immutability of the eternal one is not, for sure, the same thing as our own fixity. Since in any case we have to stammer when speaking of God, I prefer to pray with the Bible's anthropomorphisms than with the rough approximations of the philosophers.

Petitionary prayer
for the Mecca pilgrimage

With you every guest finds a meal; every caravan provisions for the way; every visitor is honored; every beggar receives what he asks; whoever hopes is rewarded; whoever seeks your goods obtains his share; you make yourself near to all who desire you, and you fill all those who turn to you.

So we stand before you in this sanctuary, hoping for your blessings. Do not disappoint, O God, the hope we have placed in you, O our Lord and master.

When Jesus tells us, *"Ask, and you shall receive,"* that certainly means that things are going to change. Otherwise, he would be mocking us. If we really are free, we do make something happen with God. And to reply that it was all foreseen from all eternity is only an escape-hatch when facing the mystery of mysteries: God loves us.

Third objection: "At any rate," someone will say, "I prayed and prayed, and nothing happened."

My reply: nobody ever has a right to say that. Why not? Because we have no way of measuring two things; first, whether we have really prayed, with what sort of faith and with how much perseverance.

Next, to judge of God's action, what measuring lines do we have? A very beautiful passage from Marcel Legaut describes very accurately the prudent judgments we can form on the effectiveness of our prayer.

"Like every other result of Providence's action, the effectiveness of our prayers can be calculated neither by observation from outside nor by experience from within, but only by faith. One can interpret the granting of a prayer and the consequences of a Providential intervention, but this must remain something personal. To say: God wants this or that; God did this or that, can be an act of impiety.

"The discovery of the efficacy of prayer is tied in with the progress of our interior life and of our faith. Little by little we find out that prayer is our most powerful, our most intense action, because there we work in closest collaboration with God. And this will be our last action when we die."

To say: "nothing changed, and so nothing will ever change," is like poison for our petitions. And it is such a great mistake. God can always change everything. The good thief sighed *"Jesus, remember me when you enter upon your reign!"* and he received the most amazing reply, promising an instantaneous change; *"This day you will be with me in paradise"* (Lk 23:42-43).

My petition re-makes me a virgin. By acting with confidence I leave behind me my past and my conditioning.

I immediately begin a future life; I am already another person. A sixty-year-old man once told me: "I've ruined my whole life." That "whole life" is totally wrong. The essential thing in our life is always ahead of us, not behind us. "If you pray," I assured him, "you are brand new, and you will start up a new life."

—And what about abandonment to God's will? What do you make of *that*? Life is what God wills; why should we ask that things should change?

True enough. There is one kind of abandonment which is a marvelous silent prayer. But we need to pay close attention to the other realities which lie just next door. Abandonment can run very close to quietism.

When we abandon ourselves to God's will we want to accomplish that will very actively; to be very creative about it; hence we must often play the role of beggars. Without constant awareness life swallows us up and sweeps us away. Awareness means initiative, reopening questions, taking our responsibilities. These are all things which reveal our poverty to us, and urge us to present our petitions to God.

—Well, what about the famous passage in St. Matthew (6:25-34). *"Your heavenly Father knows all that you need before you ask him."* Is this not a call for self-abandonment, and against asking?

This passage is not against asking; it is against worry. *Be not solicitous.* There is a pagan solicitude; but there is also a Christian way of seeking, which Jesus mentions in verse 33, which is the key to the whole passage: *"Seek first his kingship over you . . . and all these things will be given you besides."*

—So, we don't need to pray.

Oh, yes we do! Whoever really tries this "seek first the kingdom" quickly comes to realize his helplessness; and prays . . . as he had never prayed before; but his prayer is a purified prayer, on a very exalted level. In fact, if we are heard when we ask God for the grace of seeking his kingdom first in all things, we shall penetrate into the land of true holiness.

What kind of answers?

After these attempts to respond to objections which are often heard, I hope that now we can take up very directly the basic question about impetratory prayer. After all, what does it mean to be heard, when it seems to happen so seldom? What kind of answers do we get?

Answer: we are talking about an adjustment with God. This presents two aspects: replying to our request, God will come close to us; and by asking, we come close to him.

To begin with, then: God takes up our request.

I am thinking of the commonest petitions: relief from pain; light to make a decision; strength to pardon an injury; reconciliation for a couple. . . . Could we even go so far as to ask for good weather for a picnic, or for success in an examination? Yes, provided that we keep a few things very clear.

Every prayer is answered, in one way or another. God accepts the movement of our petition and answers our confidence and needs as he sees fit. To pray to him at every instant means that we love him at every instant. Then one lives with him on a familiar level, which perhaps we have mostly lost by our sophisticated sneers at the naive people who still practice prayer of petition.

Sometimes God grants right away the most childlike prayer. One well-known example is that of the snow which St. Therese of Lisieux had hoped for on the day she took the habit. A snowfall on January 10 was perhaps not a full-fledged miracle, but the way she tells it, it was something unusual just the same.

I realize perfectly well, of course, that here I am venturing onto a mine field; but I have seen the harm that skepticism and mockery have done in this area dealing with cures: from the people who live in dread of cancer to the requests inscribed on intention lists: "Lord, make my daughter's family stay together."

To brutally debunk intercessory prayer in its humblest manifestations, its most trusting expressions, means tearing God away from hearts that have no protection.

And we do this in the name of what contrary experience? For we are talking about experiences. Did those who attack petitionary prayer ever really ask for anything? What can they know about this argument from the "facts" if they themselves have never engaged in the contest of confidence? "Give me . . . cure me . . . cure him . . ."

It is all right to ask for ponderation when publicizing so-called miraculous cures; but perhaps more ponderation might also be in order in the denial of such happenings. It

---

A prayer from Zaire

Blessed are you, God,
for Africa's red earth,
for the grass and the palms,
for manioc and soybeans and peanuts.

Blessed are you, God,
for the sun, the poor man's cloak,
for storms and rain which fertilize the earth.

Blessed are you, God,
for Zaire, the great river,
for sparkling springs in the valleys.

Blessed are you, God,
for the abundance of your creatures,
for antelopes and serpents, elephants and termites,
for birds, butterflies and fish.

Blessed are you, God,
for man created in your likeness;
blessed are you for the love between man and woman
by which they share in your creative power.

All fatherhood has its source in you;
all brotherhood leads to you.

---

is so difficult to discern the facts in such cases that people quickly yield to the easy solution of taking the extreme positions.

I know (and who does not?) that every believer can speak of prayers which were obviously heard; but he does not care to brag about it, and this leaves the field too easily to the frauds which seem to be talked about more frequently. And yet!

A friend was telling me that he panicked at the mere idea of having to enter a hospital for an operation. Then he found out that he might indeed have to do so.

"I drew back from the operation; I prayed and prayed as never before: 'Lord, let me not have to undergo this.' But the verdict came. I faced it peacefully and I kept that peace throughout everything that happened at the hospital. I did not think it was me; I could not recognize myself any more, coward that I was. Wasn't that an answer to my prayers?"

Just as I was writing this chapter I found in #296 of *Solidaires* an instance of granted prayer which impressed me. E. Lespinasse wrote this from Mauritius:

"To go blind at thirty is tough," said Reynolds, *"especially when you are a young married man with one baby and another on the way, and when you are a house painter by profession. At first I suffered from discouragement, total discouragement. And with that a feeling of revolt against everything. Florisse, my wife, all of a sudden had to cope with handling the two little ones and with another big baby. I moved from the bed to the easy chair, and from the easy chair to the bed. The doctors gave me no hope at all.*

"In 1980 I went to a Charismatic renewal meeting. No, there was no spectacular cure, but one of the songs they sang touched me deeply: 'Start over again at the bottom, and take Jesus for your Shepherd.' From then on I could see a sort of light at the end of the tunnel. I prayed; I asked for two favors: to see at least a little, and to have someone close to me. . . . Without realizing it, I was trying to impose

my will on the Lord. For three or four years now God has given me a great light in my heart . . . and for my companion I have my cane, my new eyes. . . . Something urges me to try, to make an effort, to go out. I now know that it was Jesus."

Was it really Jesus? We can never tell whether this man's new-found courage was a direct result of his prayer or not. I remind the reader of Marcel Legaut's advice concerning prudence cited above. But this should not go so far as the current reticence people show when speaking of prayers that were granted. "God," they say, "is not an emergency number, a Mr. Fixit. He respects secondary causes." So he does, and I am the first to admit it. But while rooting out the weeds of credulity and over-familiarity with God, we must not massacre the good grain of faith. God can make miracles. And he does.

Since here we risk falling into the danger of magic (trying to obtain from God extraordinary things without worrying about pleasing him) it is good to keep in mind the two "always's" that Jesus kept together.

"Father, you always hear me" (Jn 11:41).

"I always do what pleases him" (Jn 8:29).

To say: "Father, give us . . ." requires that we have the mentality and the behavior of sons. The request will then be granted more royally than we could have imagined. A modern-day hymn expresses well how our petitions are heard: "We wanted a lamp, and it becomes a great light; we wanted a little fire, and we get a conflagration; a little water, and it becomes a Niagara."

But who will give us eyes to see these marvels? About a certain request which we think has gone unanswered, we are perhaps both blind and deaf.

I said above that there are two aspects of how God draws near to us through our requests. First, when we call on him God comes to succor our needs and shows us a Father's tenderness, which we can never believe in too much. Secondly, our request must go up to him, and that leads us to reflect on the very nature of asking.

At first, it begins with our most external needs, and it rushes to God without thinking much about him except in a very external manner, as "the one who distributes goodies." "Have you got any of this? Then give me some."

Little by little our petitions will move away from the depth of our own concerns and will reach into God's deepest being. "Can what I desire, O my God, become yours, and enter into your views and sentiments?" This is the path of interiorization whose purpose is that we may have the same spirit that God has, which is why the last object of petitionary prayer is to obtain the Spirit (cf. Lk 11:13). That was what one militant Catholic had understood so well when he said: "we will always meet with garbage; but the Spirit can help us see it in a different light."

This "seeing in a different light" is the sign that our petition has reached God's level. We go from "what do I expect of God?" to "what does God expect of me?" And this change of viewpoint is already an answer to our prayer because it shows that we have been changed, converted.

We ask for some small favor, or for a great one, for some area of our life. If we let this request really rise to God we shall receive back from him the whole of our life in its uniqueness, which he alone, obviously, can truly know. Then he will be able to answer us in and through the changes wrought in our hearts.

Here we come to the true efficacy of petitionary prayer, pointed out in the gospel by what has been called "Johannine overkill."

Take, as an example the Samaritan woman. She told Jesus: *"Give me this water, Sir, so that I shall not grow thirsty and have to keep coming here to draw water"* (Jn 4:15). This was already an improvement over the superficial and aggressive tone she had adopted at the start; but it remained a request for material help. Jesus reached down into the depths of her true thirst. *You have had husbands, but you don't know true love.* And he lifts her up even to the adoration of the Father; what an answer to her prayer!

We find the same thing in John 6:26-27. *"You seek me,"* Jesus told the Jews, *"because you have eaten your fill of the loaves. You shall not be working for perishable food but for food that remains unto life eternal."*

And thus petitionary prayer which often wanders in the pagan plains of self-interest and magic can take off for the blue as soon as it makes us truly raise our eyes towards God. It becomes religious, and by degrees, immensely ambitious. "I choose everything," said little St. Therese. When one is in touch with God one meets up with everything God wants to give him.

2. *"Better action than prayer"*

People with active temperaments can't help thinking that prayer is time wasted, pure idleness. We must not fail to challenge this contemporary objection with its slogans: "work is prayer"; "praying is cowardly; you run towards God in order to escape from life."

There is some truth to all this. Prayer can sometimes serve as an alibi to camouflage a dread of acting, of getting one's feet wet; of going out of one's way.

More generally, it is the passion for action itself which makes people disdain prayer: "All you need to do is to remain united to God while working." This is supposing that the problem has already been solved. Precisely; the trick is to remain united with God; but how? We too quickly pass on to pictures of ourselves working, without asking the preliminary question: "Who is really working?"

There are two ways of wasting one's life: never doing anything much, and that condemns lazy-prayer; or doing anything at all, any old way; and that condemns those who consider prayer useless.

The fact is that prayer builds up the person who is trying to re-make the world. Jesus said: *"If one of you decides to build a tower, will he not first sit down"* (Lk 14:28). The peace found in prayer makes us both more lucid and more enterprising, capable of working even in the worst surroundings, because they are enlightened by hope.

A person who prays is a person plus God, as Teresa of Avila said: "Teresa alone is nothing; Teresa and three ducats is very little; but Teresa, three ducats and God is all that is needed." With the graces of enlightenment the task is better grasped. With the graces of fortitude the one who prays can brag like St. Paul, *"When I am powerless, it is then that I am strong"* (2 Cor 12:10).

But why should we stop to pray when we are straining to press forward? For three reasons:

— as a Christian I must bring to all my tasks something more than my push and my generosity. In my action itself I want to be another Christ, revealing God. This kind of dynamism will not just happen and will not be reinvigorated save by prayer.

— I want to keep in touch with God so as to place myself firmly within his plans, and to collaborate with him.

— Prayer will keep on converting me; and what a benefit that is for the work I do, be it easy or hard, pleasant or distasteful. I will be able to remain peaceful, optimistic, and a good companion.

"Better work than pray" is a false slogan to begin with, when those who repeat it are trying to make you believe that prayer is not very useful; but sometimes prayer is classified under the heading of laziness, which certainly makes some folks look at it askance. This is a type of ignorance which I find hard to countenance. Not long ago some friends to whom I was saying that I was about to start my annual retreat, replied with a cry wrung from their hearts: "So, you are going to take a rest!" Perhaps I was wrong in contenting myself with a mere smile, instead of showing them what a tough task those days of prayer were going to be.

One also hears: "Praying is cowardly; it is better to roll up one's sleeves and count on one's efforts." I say to myself: "If you only knew that prayer is asking God to hire us to work on his job." That's when one has to begin rolling up his sleeves!

3. "Better to devote oneself to others than to pray"

Prayer can be selfish, and can reinforce selfishness; why deny it? Some people seek God alone in prayer to escape (more or less consciously) from the hardships found in every kind of fraternal living. Prayer obviously fascinates the narcissistic personalities all wrapped up in their own problems; and fearing the perils of dialogue, they take refuge in their solitude and silence.

Praying can also become a selfish protection against involvement. "I will pray for you" sometimes means: "I can't be bothered to help." Today's universal prayer as we have it on Sundays can be, if one does not strongly react, a very selfish form of prayer. All this praying for all the misfortunes found in the world can leave us totally unconcerned. We pray for peace, but on leaving church we take up again the same ill feelings we harbored on entering. We pray for the famine victims, but we don't write even a little check.

But, after duly denouncing this possible deviation in prayer without service to others, we must now question the inverse deviation, much more common and more appealing: "I want to do all I can; that is worth more than any prayer."

True, caring for others does not turn us from God. But are we so sure that we are truly caring? In the very interesting "Alliance Magazine" I found this passage in a meditation which shows that instead of thinking "God or others?" it is more profitable to question ourselves about "God in my life with others." A woman I know, a wife, mother of four, and a sociologist, prays over Matthew 25:42. *"I was hungry and you gave me no food."*

"Provoked by Matthew, I think of that beggar whom I saw in the subway. I did not share anything with him, even though I have said to myself once for all that it is better to give rather than to risk turning my back on someone in distress. Sometimes I see the face of a friend, who has no one but me, and I have not written to her;

"It's up to me to be Nana Mouskouri"

It seems to me that more and more people need love, much love, love that can be seen and felt. But they want it to be easy, effortless, starting from the slightest desire.

In the United States, for instance, people are coming to want to buy God, just as they buy everything else. In fact, the sects offer fellowship and religion very cheap. Or again, people calculate what believing in God is worth to them.

Sometimes people ask me: "What has God done for you?" I answer that he gave me my life, but that it is up to me to be Nana Mouskouri. Then others tell me: "I was sick, and he gave me back my health."

That can turn into a sort of business deal. I break a leg; if God heals me I shall believe in him.

No! for me faith is not that at all. Of course, it will happen that I may say, "My God, make this succeed." But I shan't stop believing if it doesn't succeed. What do I know about how God thinks of success? Perhaps it is a big success when I have fought hard, when I did not get discouraged. That too is something he gives me; I don't get discouraged. I think that believing in him means doing enough so that he may believe in me.

*sometimes I think of the messages of Amnesty Internation-
al that have piled up on my desk. Or I think of that family
conversation in which I was not able to guess at the
unformulated request which lay beneath the commonplaces
exchanged; or I think of such and such a colleague, isolated
because he has not been invited."*

"Provoked by Matthew"! What would become of
service to others, very generous at the start, without the
provocation afforded by the gospel? I know (I have been
told this often enough) that "giving of oneself is the true
gospel lesson, the best way to contact God, the surest kind
of mental prayer." True; but I can't help thinking of St.
Vincent de Paul, of Mother Teresa, of this or that fellow
priest wearing himself out . . . and how those people pray!

It's easy to say: "I prefer to devote myself." But do we
really do it? And how do we do it? There is such a thing
as weariness in loving, such a thing as self-seeking in one's
very devotedness. And above all, the call to love "as Jesus
loved" sooner or later brings us up short before closed
doors. Then, if we want to keep on loving anyhow, cost
what it may, prayer cannot be far off; otherwise we just
quit.

Yet the slogans are hard to drown out. "Love alone
counts and suffices." Yes, but what kind of love? "I find
God in others; that's my prayer." Very good; but can I ask
you a couple of questions? Who else do you find there?
Don't you make a choice? Don't you ever drop any of
them? And how do you meet them? Is there any in-depth
encounter and listening? What do you have to give them?
You think you are finding God in them, but what God?
What God do you reveal to them?

To answer all these questions, how badly we need prayer!

4. *"Distractions prevent me from praying"*

The commonest and most wearying struggle in prayer
comes from distractions. When one mentions them one
thinks right away about mental prayer, which is in fact

their favorite stomping-ground: solitude, silence, an empty mind . . . and there they are—some very normal and others perfectly fantastic. At times one can't help saying: "how on earth did I get *here*?"

Still, we mustn't totally neglect the problem of distractions in other types of prayer. Every prayer requires attention for it to be worthy of God and beneficial to ourselves. We need to examine our attentiveness in saying the rosary, the Office, and even at Mass.

It was especially with mental prayer in mind that I put together these ten anti-distraction counsels, of which the tenth is perhaps the most apt to tranquillize our minds.

1) Don't mistake your simple inner "moving picture show" for mental prayer. This is just daydreaming. Praying means praying. Certain suggestions such as "don't concern yourself about your distractions" need to be tightened up, otherwise we run the risk of compromising the seriousness of our prayer.

2) Don't start your prayer when you are already distracted. There has to be a break first: a placing of yourself in God's presence. (This can be very brief: "you are here, and I am here.")

3) Pay attention to bodily posture. The position taken does not matter too much provided we keep all the firmness and dignity we can. When possible, an erect backbone is the best attitude to take before God, the one least prone to distractions. (This is the great trick of the Za-Zen practitioners.)

4) Accept one's problems, be they passing or habitual, with regard to one's lack of concentration. We have to pray with what we have; a little humility is no handicap here.

5) But it is not a bad idea to use modern practices to reach deeper recollection. These fit in with the nervosity, the distractedness and the superficiality which are the banes of modern living. If we struggle against these pitfalls we shall probably find ourselves less distracted in mental prayer or during the liturgy.

6) Especially during mental prayer, the best way to

control distractions is to use the strategy of driving one presence out by introducing another. The main point is to remain active so as to receive what God may wish to give us: peace, light, sentiments — and hence to be filled with his presence which by itself will drive out the presence of the distractions. "You want me to fill you" says God through St. Augustine, "but you are already filled up." Hence one should prefer this positive action in favor of God rather than a negative and direct assault against distractions. Saying, "I will not be distracted" risks keeping us distracted, whereas, "I want your presence" gently and indirectly drives away the intruders. The idea is not to empty oneself, but fill oneself. And above all we must not wait until we of our own efforts have emptied ourselves before filling ourselves with God. It is his presence itself which creates the vacuum.

7) Never abandon prayer, whatever state we may be in. Give up the notion of achieving an ideal prayer. What counts is to keep on willing to pray. That is all the Lord expects of us: "I do want to pray." Remain in that disposition, and seek obstinately the double presence: to ourselves, and to God. Compared with this huge determination (proved by sacrifices of our time, our preferences, our attitudes) distractions are only little botherations, and even occasions for making acts of love: "You see, Lord, how much I prefer you to all this nonsense."

8) What should we think about "mantras"? By this is meant two or three syllables which permit us to utilize the principle of presence against presence. Pronounced mentally, without any effort, the mantra gently does away with distractions, simply by being there. It is a good prelude to opening us up to God's presence.

9) Be wary especially of worries. These can be very legitimate (a sick child, for instance) but also, and very often they are attacks of self-love arising out of deficient confidence in God. They are very difficult to conciliate with mental prayer. We should decide that at least during this time given to God we are going to trust him entirely for

everything, and to open ourselves so wide to his presence that our Father will then help us to live aright with our justified worries, and to dissipate the harmful ones.

10) "If all you did during your whole hour of mental prayer was to take your heart as firmly as you can, and present it to our Lord, even if every time you did this your heart would turn aside again, your hour would be very well spent" (St. Francis de Sales to Mme. de Ballon, 1617).

5. "I haven't got time"

"No time to pray" is perhaps the most dangerous modern objection against prayer, because it is accepted without any argument. Some day a person who up to then used to pray, recognizes that he or she no longer does so; and if you question them they say: "I don't have time any more." To them this seems so obvious, so decisive, that no further discussion is possible. Yet it should certainly be discussed.

People think: "If I had time, I would like to pray." Or, "I am going to retire soon; then I'll have time to pray." And what Christian has not said to himself: "At least, during vacation time, I shall be able to pray."

No. People who no longer pray for lack of time seldom take up prayer again when they do have time. It is not all that simple. Lack of time kills off only the prayer which is already anemic. The cure lies not in consulting our agenda or the clock, but in questioning our desire to pray.

Wisdom affirms that people always find the time for what they really want to do. I too, for a long time, gave up mental prayer protesting indignantly: "But where do you want me to find an hour, or even a half-hour every morning?" I did find it, though; but only after I had been won over to mental prayer.

Forgetting my own experience, when someone sought to prove to me that he did not have time to pray, and if he seemed sincere, I tried with his permission to look into how he was using his time. Silly me! Now I see more clearly the three stages in a return to prayer (not that I think they are easy stages!). First, arouse the desire to pray; then start praying again, and finally worry about the time to do it.

1) Arouse the desire to pray

We must not consider prayer as one duty to be filed away among a lot of others. People did this for the obligation of hearing Mass; and when the law seemed to become less stringent we saw a lot of them giving up what they had never really loved.

Prayer has too often been presented as a duty, whereas it is a question of love. Some accused themselves of forgetting their prayers or saying them badly. When a lover forgets his rendezvous or pleads a lack of time, that should ring a bell; his love is languishing. When a Christian no longer can find time to pray, what he needs to look for is not time, but love.

Prayer is not one thing more or one thing less in our lives. It is my whole life which I must give back to God. "You have made us for yourself," said St. Augustine. In its myriad forms, prayer is this going back to God. Without love we can play at praying, but that prayer will never last.

Here are some questions which may provoke thought in a Christian: "What are you doing with your life? What do you want to do with it? Do you not feel that you are growing apart from God and living more and more without him?"

2) Encourage people to "take the plunge"

These questions may possibly incite someone to pray, but the classical danger remains: to stay on the river bank instead of diving headlong into the water.

"It is really ridiculous," writes Fr. Besnard, "how many Christians, priests and religious know nothing about prayer save a sterile nostalgia. It is something they inquire about in all its details, but which they are incapable of really getting their teeth into."

As always, the first steps beyond theory will cost some-

How to incite people to pray

During a parish meeting on prayer, a group chose to reflect on a question too seldom considered: how can we spread a taste for prayer? I listed ten ideas which I found useful.

- We awaken prayer by praying.

- Feel responsible for the prayer of others.

- Foresee the objections.

- Don't be afraid to talk about prayer. Reticence is nice, but witnessing is nicer.

- Don't hesitate to say what prayer has given you. For instance, it brings peace; it takes away negative attitudes; it gives a calm audacity, the desire and the means of holding to God's will.

- Become familiar with the Bible.

- Learn how to discern God in events.

- Suggest common prayers, and form prayer groups.

- Don't connect prayer with boredom and ugliness, especially with the young. Visit beautiful churches; show beautiful icons.

- Listen to people's difficulties in prayer.

thing; one would prefer to read yet another book about methods, and so on. But many examples prove that a return to prayer is at your fingertips: go ahead and pray! It does not matter how or when; but dive in. Start praying again.

3) Reflect on time

Taking up prayer again will be a good opportunity for us to revise our notions about time. How defeatist it is to keep on crying: "We are living the lives of lunatics!" Overloaded agendas, neurotic glances at our watches, agitation, and then the narcotic of TV, the endless conversations . . . all this is not using time, but wasting it.

Prayer will make us use our time in a more intense manner, and with greater calm. It is not true prayer unless it is well done, and in this way it will re-introduce us into the flow of time which we have mastered. It teaches us, not to do everything, but to do right what we undertake. Self-possession and contact with God, mental prayer will teach us once again how to welcome everything and how to be present to it, to "be there" which is the only manner of living worthy of a human being.

The more we take time to pray, the more powerfully will we live. That is no slogan; it's the universal testimony given by the great adopts of prayer.

We need only to think of the time we waste through nervousness or laziness, through routine and robot-like superficiality. Today it is not easy to be at once constantly alert, yet calm; open, and interiorly occupied. Finally, we live our lives any old way, with a few rich moments which make us define what time might be if it were fully enriched, as they talk of "enriched uranium."

Well, prayer can do that for us. It is pure oxygen; it calms and arouses, it makes us both attentive to others and ready to go back down into our soul's depths.

No doubt, it calls for us to give it some of our time, but it will make of us the kind of people of whom others say; "How can someone so creative remain so unruffled?"

And now, after all this discussion which may have

seemed very theoretical, I would like to repeat that we are, on the contrary, invited to start practicing immediately. Dive in! *God gives the gift of prayer to the one who prays!*

THIRTY MINUTES FOR GOD

"A busy priest comments on how he returned to daily prayer after giving it up for some time, and on many other aspects of and questions about a prayer life in the modern world. Short, conversational chapters talk about real prayer as opposed to routine, uninspired putting-in-time prayer. His main point: '. . .Either hunger for God is the sun around which I organize everything; or else God is just one object among others orbiting the very crowded sky of my life' " (*Spiritual Book News*).

Series: Spirituality
ISBN 0-911782-49-4, paper, 5 $\frac{1}{8}$ x 8, 127 pp.

MY LIFE WITH JESUS

"Our spiritual lives will always benefit from a return to the source of our Christianity, the gospels that tell the story of Jesus of Nazareth. Well-known journalist Andre Seve here offers us his own reflections and meditations on the four gospels, the way each shows a different facet of Jesus' life and belief and how this can affect our lives and spirituality. . . . We will find comfort as well as challenge here. Father Seve's reflections are fresh and personal and yet they can suggest directions for the reader's own exploitations" (*Spiritual Book News*).

Series: Spirituality
ISBN 0-911782-52-4, paper, 5 $\frac{1}{8}$ x 8, 208 pp.